8

GW00634436

foulsham

LONDON • NEW YORK • TORONTO • SYDNEY

foulsham

The Publishing House, Bennetts Close, Cippenham,
Berkshire, SL1 5AP, England

For Caroline

ISBN 0-572-02609-9

Copyright © 2000 Richard B

Cover photograph © Britsto

LEWISHAM	
Cypher	28.8.01
155.9042	£7.99
557112	8

Neither the editors of W. Foulsham & Co. Ltd nor the
author nor the publisher take responsibility for any
possible consequences from any treatment, procedure,
test, exercise, action or application of medication or
preparation by any person reading or following the
information in this book. The publication of this book
does not constitute the practice of medicine, and this
book does not attempt to replace any diet or
instructions from your doctor. The author and
publisher advise the reader to check with a doctor
before administering any medication or undertaking
any course of treatment or exercise.

Printed in Great Britain by St. Edmundsbury Press, Bury St. Edmunds, Suffolk.

contents

about the author

Richard Brennan is a fully qualified teacher of the Alexander technique, having undergone a three-year teacher training course approved by the Society of Teachers of the Alexander Technique; he travels throughout Europe giving talks and courses on the technique. He has been featured in several newspapers and magazines including *Cosmopolitan, Hello* and *Home and Country*; he has appeared on BBC 1 and RTE 1 and been featured on BBC Radios 4 and 5. He lives in Galway, Ireland where he runs a private practice; he is also the director of an Alexander teacher training course in Ireland.

Other Books by Richard Brennan: *Alexander Technique – New Perspectives; The Alexander Technique – A Practical Introduction; The Alexander Technique Manual; Mind and Body Stress Relief with the Alexander Technique.*

acknowledgements

Firstly, I wish to express my sincere thanks to my wife Caroline for her support in looking after the family while I was writing, and for her help with proof reading as well!

Secondly, to all those who helped me research the book – to Mary Irwin for her great help and suggestions about aromatherapy; to Marian Brady for her kindness and help with the section on acupuncture; to Jane Totterham for her help in checking through the section on homeopathy; to Stefan Ball who looked through the section on Bach flower remedies; to Veronica O'Neil for her help with T'ai Chi and to Simon Abbot who sent me facts about shiatsu all the way from Tobago.

Thirdly, to all those who edited and were involved in the publishing and publication of the book – to Lucy Ackroyd who looked through the first draft; to my editor, Wendy Hobson, for helping to make the project as stress-free as possible from beginning to end; and to all those at Foulsham Publishing who worked so hard behind the scenes.

introduction

On 3 October 1999 when I visited the BBC news website I was met with the headline 'Stress Tops Work Sickness League'. This article went on to say that stress is now the number one reason behind absence from work – overtaking the common cold and backache. The article revealed that over one third of employers are now providing stress counselling for their employees because they are increasingly worried about the impact stress can have on their business.

A 1999 report by business information group Gee Publishing UK claims that one in five companies with more than 1,000 staff consider stress to be a 'major problem'. The report, which surveyed more than 300 organisations, found that a growing number of managers are being trained how to recognise and reduce stress. Some companies are even issuing employees with booklets on how to cope with stress.

Yet, rather than just *coping* with stress it is vital to find ways to reduce or eliminate stress from our lives. There are effective complementary methods of reducing the physical, mental and emotional tension that can build up when we are under stress. Many of the physical problems from which we suffer today can be easily avoided if we just learn to look after ourselves in a caring way. This book aims directly to counter the detrimental effects of our increasingly stressful lifestyles. It will be particularly helpful to those who have an erratic or traumatic emotional life at home, or to those who face deadline after deadline at work, or even to those who simply feel that life itself is hardly worth living.

Although stress may lead to a wide variety of illnesses, it is not an illness itself – it is a habit of life: a habit that many people get into and one that we can get out of. The aim of this book is to offer practical help if you are one of those millions of people who feel that they are caught in a vicious cycle of stress and strain, and find it hard to switch off from the ever-increasing pressures of modern life.

My purpose in writing this book is to put forward a different choice; another way of being; a different and happier way of life to the one so many people feel trapped by. I will explain not only how the different complementary health techniques can alleviate physical stress, but how you can help yourself to reduce mental and emotional stress as well. You will find the information in this book particularly helpful if you are suffering from stress-related conditions such as depression, panic attacks, high blood pressure, anxiety or just frequent periods of irritability. The great philosophers Socrates, Plato and Hippocrates all realised that there is an inseparable unity between the body, mind and emotions; therefore it follows that mental stress will lead to physical tension and emotional instability, and vice versa.

Over the past few decades human beings have changed their environment far more than at any other time in history. Dramatic technological advancements may have alleviated hunger and the struggle for survival for many, yet people today seem more stressed and far less contented than the 'simpler' people of previous generations. Upon reflection it is clear that the increasing pace of life is having a harmful effect on a great many people, and today many of us are under a great deal more pressure, both at work and at home, than ever before. There no longer seems to be enough time to enjoy the simple things in life, and as a result, ill health, unhappiness and worry often significantly affect the quality of life.

To find answers in our search for a less stressful life, does not mean that we have to return to the caves or trees in search of a more primitive existence. What we need is to find different ways of reacting to our situation so that stress levels are kept to a minimum. Throughout this book, therefore, I hope to present you with the choice of achieving a happier and less pressured way of life.

1

recognising stress

*'I try to take to take one day
at a time – but sometimes several
days attack me at once.'*
ASHLEIGH BRILLIANT

Stress today

We are living in stressful times: computers, faxes, e-mail and mobile phones all encourage us to act, and react, faster and faster. Most of us can cope with stress in the short-term, but when we have to endure that same stress over long periods it can be harmful to us both physically and mentally.

Although 'improving the quality of life' appears to be an objective that we all share, it seems that with all the scientific, medical and technological 'progress' humankind has made over the last century, many people are no happier now than in previous generations. Despite our various efforts to find a happier and more contented way of living, the enjoyable times we experience are becoming less frequent and shorter in duration the more we 'progress'.

Today, so many of us are rushing around trying to keep appointments, meet deadlines or reach impossible targets, that being stressed has become the 'normal' way to live. So, despite all our obvious material advancements and the freedom from many diseases given by recent medical advances, people are now suffering from a new affliction – chronic stress. Surely to measure our quality of life we must include our physical, emotional and mental states and not only our material comforts.

Life is not an emergency

It is vital not to underestimate the many effects that stress can have on our lives, which can permeate our whole existence until we can reach a point where we feel life is hardly worth living. Stress can affect us physically in such a way that our whole system is constantly on 'red alert', causing pain and discomfort in our joints and muscles. It can result in stress-related illnesses such as strokes and heart problems, which are major causes of death in the developed world. Stress can affect us mentally by causing the mind to be over-active, giving little or no control over persistent unwanted thoughts, often resulting in endless worry for no reason. It influences us emotionally because we can lose control of our anger and act irrationally, which eventually may damage relationships with family or friends. It also can affect us spiritually, because it takes us away from the peace and tranquillity that is the essence of who we are. The effects of chronic stress can be very damaging and the root cause needs to be understood in order to reduce these harmful effects.

At first, we may take pleasure from the adrenaline 'buzz' as we take on exciting new projects and challenges, but in the long term stress can deprive us of everything that is important. How often do we stop for even a moment to ask ourselves whether the path we have taken in life is actually making us more satisfied – and if not, why not? Sometimes it may be necessary to be willing to challenge our own preconceived assumptions. Even though it is obvious that we now live longer and are far more efficient than we used to be, when you add joy and fulfilment into the equation, it is not at all clear that we have really achieved a better quality of life.

When under stress our whole muscular system remains on red alert.

An increasing number of people are visiting their doctors when they find themselves seduced into a spiral of speed and stress which can manifest itself in chronic muscle tension, acute anxiety, fidgety or restless behaviour, or a distinct lack of peace of mind. Sleeping tablets, beta-blockers and antidepressants are given out at an alarming rate but we need to find healthier answers that do not rely on the use of potentially addictive drugs, many of which have unpleasant side-effects or can lose their effect when taken consistently over a period of time. Just take a moment to look at these facts:

- In the USA heart disease is increasing by 100 per cent every ten years.

- In the UK 250,000 people die every year from heart attacks.

- In the USA 16,000 tons of aspirin and over 5 billion tranquillisers are consumed each year.

- In the UK over 40 million working days are lost every year through illness directly related to stress. The cost to British industry is estimated at £1.5 billion each year.

- In the USA the annual estimated medical cost of stress is over $1 billion.

- Over 50 per cent of marriages in the USA and 40 per cent in the UK end in divorce.

If we feel stressed during our working day, adrenaline – which causes the brain to be in a state of excitation – remains in our system for many hours or even days afterwards, and as a result we are likely to have less patience than usual. The increase in stress at work over recent years correlates closely with the number of marital problems and the high divorce rates we see today.

City life

Today, over half of the world population lives in cities and has to cope with the incessant noise, pollution, overcrowded living conditions and traffic congestion that accompany city life. We live in a strange society in which money has become more important than people's health or education, and where friendliness is often viewed with suspicion. Many of us are becoming more and more dehumanised as we stare at a computer or television screen for a large proportion of our lives. Over 40 per cent of homes in the UK have more than one television and the average family in USA has the television switched on for more than eight hours a day. These activities reduce our awareness of our environment and have a detrimental effect on social skills.

Being constantly stimulated can become an ingrained habit, to the point where people become restless, nervous or worried when there is nothing to do. Intrusive advertisements and flashing lights in cities and on television demand our attention and over-stimulate our neuro-muscular system: it has now become the deliberate policy of many television companies to increase the volume of sound during commercial breaks, making them even more intrusive. When we suffer from over-stimulation, just waiting for the lift or being in a queue at the supermarket may be all it takes to annoy us. The sad thing is that many people now believe that this is normal human behaviour. Like so many other habits, this is a hard one to break and determination is needed if we are to free ourselves from the invisible chains that bind us so tightly.

Many of us have forgotten how to relax and enjoy life, and this we must do if we are ever to have a chance of being contented. When we are under stress we can no longer think clearly or objectively, because we are often reacting subconsciously to all the stimuli to which we are subjected, and as a result, we begin to lose touch with the elements in life that could make us happy. As an Alexander technique teacher, what always amazes me is that many people who are living under tremendous pressures, both at work and in their personal relationships, are oblivious to exactly how much stress they are under until their body starts to go wrong. A great many people have forgotten how to relax and are unaware of the fact.

Causes of stress

In order to start combating stress, it is essential to understand what causes it and to understand what it is doing to our bodies and minds. The external causes of stress are many and varied, and its effects will be moderated by our individual nature, constitution and past experiences. When discussing stress, it is therefore helpful to consider the distinction between external and internal factors.

External factors

The external factors causing stress include the many outside stimuli that bombard our senses. We are not always aware that certain external events are causing stress – for example we may feel agitated when road workers are using very loud machinery, but it is not until the noise stops and we feel relief that we realise that we were disturbed. External factors include:

Major life events

These include the death of a spouse, close friend or relative, separation or divorce, legal proceedings, personal injury or accident, starting or losing a job, pregnancy or the birth of a baby, attending a new school, moving house and so on.

Physical environment

This includes anything unpleasant that we experience through our five senses, such as bright or flashing lights, loud or strange noises, heat or cold, unpleasant tastes or smells, or confined places.

Daily problems

Traffic congestion, losing important documents or keys, cars or household appliances not working, parking or speeding tickets all fall into this category. Often, the more stressed we are, the more likely that we will forget or lose things, and the worse we will react when we do.

Social interaction

Impolite or rude behaviour, for example while driving, can be a source of stress. The more stressed our society becomes as a whole, the more likely we are to encounter aggressive behaviour from others. If we react badly to the stress of others the situation may escalate out of all proportion, as is the case with the increasing problem of 'road rage'.

Social restrictions

These can vary from having to be on time for an appointment, being forced to meet unreasonable deadlines, or having to obey petty rules and regulations. Again, the more wound up we are, the more we will react against trivial restrictions placed on us – and vice versa.

Internal factors

Internal factors are determined by our own physiological make-up and life experiences. They include reactions to certain situations, the way we think and behave, and our own perception of life.

Personality traits

These are long-term in-built tendencies that define a person's character. Examples of these can be seen in the perfectionist, the workaholic or the person who is habitually disorganised.

Lifestyle

Our daily habits and choices determine our style of living – for example, a lack of sleep or a lack of physical exercise, an inadequate diet, too much caffeine and trying to fit too much into the day can lead to high levels of stress.

Mental perceptions

Sometimes we cause our own stress simply by the way we perceive the world about us. Examples of this can be found in those who have rigid ways of thinking, take comments too personally or have unrealistic expectations and are therefore constantly disappointed. People who have a tendency to think the worst of themselves, others or events will be more prone to stress.

Past experiences

Unresolved traumatic or stressful experiences in the past can lead to a heightened stress response when memories are triggered. For example, some people are left with a fear of abandonment after a loved one has died, or a fear of driving years after a car accident.

Response to stress

Stress and panic are normal and natural reactions to danger – they are our responses when we are afraid. It is natural to become stressed if a ferocious dog confronts you or you become separated from your child in a large crowd of people. The panic you experience is the body's pre-programmed way of reacting to the possible dangers that may arise in these situations. During this reaction, specific physiological changes take place. The adrenal glands become more active, causing the whole body to become more active, which helps us to be more alert and ready to cope with the emergency at hand. When the danger has passed, our body's functions will then gradually return to normal. This reaction is sometimes called the 'fight or flight' response and provides the body with the necessary strength, speed and stamina for survival. We are well equipped to cope with the changes that the body undergoes as long as the situation is short-lived, but we are not, it seems, designed to cope with frequent fearful experiences that occur on a daily basis over a long period of time.

In the 1930s an American doctor, Hans Selye, was one of the first to analyse in depth the human response to severe stress. He described the body's adjustment to prolonged stress as the 'general adaptation syndrome' and divided the stress response into three phases. He called them the 'alarm response phase', the 'adaptation phase' and the 'exhaustion phase'.

Alarm response phase

The alarm response is the immediate reaction to danger. This response is controlled by the endocrine system, which regulates various bodily functions including the immune system, metabolism, respiration, sex hormones and allergic responses. Stressful situations activate the endocrine glands, which include the adrenal, pituitary and hypothalamus, and these then secrete hormones into the bloodstream. These hormones are powerful stimulants that prepare you to cope with an emergency and produce the following responses:

- Increased heart rate

- Increased blood pressure

- Increased blood sugar, fats and cholesterol

- Increased breathing rate

- Increased muscle tension

- Mental alertness

- Greater sensitivity

- Perspiration.

Adaptation phase

If any stressful situation is prolonged, then the body adapts accordingly. This stage is not necessarily harmful providing the person has periods of rest and relaxation to counterbalance the tension caused during the stress response. During this stage, people may be prone to lapses in concentration, irritability, lethargy, physical tiredness and mental fatigue.

Exhaustion phase

If the stress continues over a long period, the body can no longer cope with its own defence mechanisms and the person will 'burn out'. They will suffer from adrenal exhaustion, which occurs when blood sugar levels decrease as the adrenaline supply becomes depleted. This leads to a dramatic reduction in the person's tolerance to stressful situations and soon they will be physically, mentally and emotionally exhausted. If nothing is done to redress the balance, the person will eventually become ill or even collapse.

Harmful effects of stress

There are differing opinions in the medical profession as to whether prolonged stress can be a direct cause of illness. Some doctors believe that stress can directly cause high blood pressure and an increase in the level of fatty acids in the blood, while others believe that excessive tension over a period of time causes a reduction in the body's own defence mechanisms, which indirectly causes disease. Whichever way you look at it, stress is bad for your general health and can even lead to premature death through a stroke or heart disease.

Let's take the example of the habitual reaction that arises when we are running late for an appointment. Many of us respond by tensing our whole body, hunching our shoulders, clenching our teeth or arching our back. As we fear the consequences of being late we are no longer in conscious control of our actions and may well act irrationally. If we are driving, we may even take unnecessary risks which could threaten our own or other people's lives. This in turn can make us even more stressed, creating a vicious circle. These kinds of habitual reactions eventually become so ingrained that we still have much more muscle tension that necessary even when we think we are relaxed. Fearful responses often originate from our school years, when being late resulted in some form of ridicule or punishment, and, like Pavlov's dogs, we still respond in a similar fashion many years later, even when being late for an appointment is of little importance. If this behaviour is allowed to persist over a period of time, we may end up suffering from one or other of the stress-related illnesses listed below.

Recognising the signs of stress

Although stress has very definite physical effects, such as high blood pressure or the production of specific hormones, we are usually unaware of these changes taking place in our bodies and as a result stress can go unnoticed for many months or even years. The way in which we detect stress in ourselves or others varies, but stress will often manifest itself in one of two ways: physical tension or mental and emotional symptoms.

Physical tension

If you are suffering from stress it is likely that you will also have one or more of the following physical symptoms:

PAIN WITH MUSCLE OR JOINT PROBLEMS
- Backache
- Neckache

- Headache
- Migraine

- Repetitive Strain Injury (RSI)

BLOOD CIRCULATION OR HEART PROBLEMS
- High blood pressure
- Poor circulation

- Coronary thrombosis

RESPIRATORY PROBLEMS
- Asthma
- Shallow breathing

- Hyperventilation

DIGESTIVE PROBLEMS
- Ulcers
- Heartburn

- Constipation
- Indigestion

NERVOUS PROBLEMS
- Trapped nerves
- Over-active nervous system

- Clumsiness
- Panic attacks.

Mental and emotional symptoms

The three most common conditions that accompany the physical symptoms are worry, anxiety and depression. These may be accompanied by an increase in smoking or drinking, a change of sleeping pattern and a lack of interest in sex. Other symptoms include:

WORRY

- Restlessness
- Uncontrolled thoughts
- Irritability
- Indecisiveness
- Tendency to talk about self and problems

ANXIETY

- Inability to relax
- Tendency to panic
- Feeling of being on edge
- Poor memory
- Nervousness
- Tenseness

DEPRESSION

- Tiredness or exhaustion
- Pessimism
- Erratic mood swings
- Lack of interest in anything
- Difficulty concentrating
- Apathy
- Lack of confidence in own ability.

Putting modern stress into perspective

The first step in reducing the level of stress in the body is to understand exactly what happens to us when we become stressed. In humanity's primitive state, when life was being threatened, the body's reaction to stress was extremely beneficial, as it worked to help keep the person alive when in danger. Even now, if we are in a life-threatening situation such as a near-miss while driving, the body's automatic reaction to the circumstances may save lives. But today, much of the stress we feel is not due to life-threatening situations and is therefore inappropriate.

Living in this fast-moving age, with an increasing number of targets to achieve and a feeling that everything should have been done yesterday, we feel under continual stress. It is crucial that we acquire a more relaxed way of life – for the sake of our mental and physical health, as well as our emotional well-being. During a recent trip to the South Pacific Islands, I noticed that few people wore watches and the whole community had a system called 'coconut time' which meant that any time given was approximate and no one was too concerned if you were late. As a result, everyone was far more relaxed, and in fact nearly everything started within ten minutes of the time stated.

The table below shows the body's major responses to stress, their initial benefits and the detrimental effect if allowed to go on too long.

Detrimental effects of prolonged stress

NATURAL RESPONSES TO STRESS	BENEFITS	DETRIMENTAL EFFECTS OVER PROLONGED PERIODS
INCREASE OF THYROID HORMONE IN THE BLOODSTREAM	Speeds up the body's metabolism providing extra energy to cope with the emergency at hand	Can lead to insomnia and exhaustion. May also cause an intolerance to heat and extreme nervousness
RELEASE OF CORTISONE FROM THE ADRENAL GLANDS	Protects the body from an allergic reaction such as asthma	Destroys the body's resistance to infections so that the ability to fight off illnesses is impaired. Makes bones more brittle so that they are more prone to fracture. Dramatically reduces the stomach's resistance to its own acid and can lead to gastric and duodenal ulcers
RELEASE OF ENDORPHINES FROM THE HYPOTHALAMUS	Kills pain so that the person under stress does not feel injuries until after the danger has past (a similar effect to morphine)	Depletes the levels of endophins in the body and can aggravate painful conditions such as migraines, backaches, headaches and arthritis
RELEASE OF SUGAR INTO THE BLOODSTREAM, PRODUCING AN INCREASE IN THE INSULIN LEVEL	Provides a short-lived energy supply to escape from a situation quickly	Makes excessive demands on the pancreas for insulin and can bring about or aggravate diabetes

Natural responses to stress	Benefits	Detrimental Effects over prolonged periods
Increase of cholesterol in the blood	Gives the muscles energy over a prolonged period of stress	Can cause hardening of the arteries, which may contribute to heart attacks
Increase in rate of heart-beat	Pumps the blood faster to give the body more energy	Causes hypertension (high blood pressure) which could lead to strokes or heart attacks
Rapid breathing	Supplies the blood with extra oxygen	Encourages shallow breathing, which puts other systems in the body under stress
Thickening of the blood	Creates a greater capacity in the blood to carry oxygen, slows down bleeding from a wound and helps to fight infections	Increases the risk of heart attacks and strokes
Increase in the activity of the sweat gland	Cools down the body, which is hotter from over-exertion	Causes over sweating
More acute sight, hearing, touch, taste and smell	Ensures that all the senses are functioning at their optimum to aid survival	Dulls the senses after a stressful situation which means that errors can easily occur

As you can see short-term stress is not harmful and can even be beneficial – it is when you have been under stress for a while that it becomes a problem. The simple stress-reducing exercises and procedures described later in this book can help you to become a happier, more conscious and less stressed human being. The advice given in this book will help you to examine your life and to make the necessary changes to assist you in living in a more harmonious way. Remember that at the end of their life no one says 'I wish I had spent more time at the office' or 'I wish I had reached those business targets'.

2

reducing stress levels

*'There's only one corner of the
universe you can be certain of
improving and that's your own self.'*
ALDOUS HUXLEY

Muscle tension

Over-tense muscles can have a devastating effect on our posture, how we move and the functioning of all our internal systems. If we are suffering from stress, we will be less likely to notice this build up of muscle tension until we find ourselves afflicted with a 'sudden' illness. This is because when we are busy trying to cope with the pressures of life we give ourselves little time to be aware of our bodies.

Our bodies, in fact, give us plenty of warning that things are not as they should be, but usually we either ignore the signs or are completely oblivious to them. You often hear people say that they 'don't have time to be ill' – but if we push ourselves to the limits we must expect the consequences. The most common warning sign that all is not well is pain and once we are in pain the body tenses up even more. Many people find themselves in this vicious circle which can, at best, be only temporarily relieved by conventional medical treatment.

Although stress often starts in the mind, it is instantly transmitted to the body in the form of muscular tension, which is then reinforced over the years until even simple movements become a strain. This excessive muscular tension, which can be present during every activity we perform, often has its roots in childhood; as a result, it feels so normal that it would seem strange to be without it. Many of us have become accustomed to experiencing a certain degree of stress all the time, and even people who think they are relaxed often carry far more tension than they realise. Stress is self-perpetuating, because the more stress we are under during the course of our daily activities the more tense our muscles become, and the more tense our muscles are the more likely we are to become stressed, even when we are faced with small problems.

Reducing muscle tension

One of the first important steps in reducing stress is to become conscious of how tense your muscles are and then set about releasing this tension. You can begin to do this by stopping completely and becoming aware of the muscular tension you are holding even when you are supposedly doing nothing. Many people are very surprised when they begin to feel how tight their muscles have become. Self-awareness is the basic tool which will help you to relieve many of the ailments that life's stresses and strains have produced. It is not until you become aware of your muscular tension that you really can do anything about it. Indira Gandhi once said 'you must learn to be still in the midst of activity and to be vibrantly alive in repose.' The following exercises will help you to do just this.

Exercise one – slowing down

This exercise will help you to slow down and actively enable you to let go of muscle tension. At first, many people who are stressed find these exercises difficult as their mind is racing with all the thoughts of what they 'should' be doing. If you are one of these people, try not to get disillusioned. Give yourself ten to fifteen minutes at least once a day for a week or so. If you persevere it does get easier. At first, ten minutes may feel like a long time, but as you begin to relax it will seem shorter.

The exercise can be done either sitting or lying down – whichever feels more comfortable. It is important to get in contact with how you are feeling and what you are thinking as your emotions will invariably affect levels of stress within you body.

Choose a quiet time of day when you can be alone. It does not matter whether it is early in the morning, during the day or in the evening. Spend ten minutes focusing on your body; you can start with your feet and work upwards. As you are aware of your feet try to release any tension you can feel in the toes or ankles. Continue up the whole length of your body. Take as much time as you feel you need with any particular part of your body. Do not get irritated if your mind wanders off on to other thoughts – just gently bring it back to the present moment by re-focusing your attention.

Once your body has relaxed as much as possible, practise being an observer of your body, mind and emotions; try to make no judgement on what you are feeling or thinking. Ask yourself:

1. How am I feeling? Do I feel happy, sad, joyful, miserable, angry or any other emotion? Perhaps you are feeling a lack of emotion. Try not to judge any emotion that you are feeling – there is no such thing as a bad emotion, even though we may have a negative reaction to certain emotions.

2. Where does my mind wander off to? Do I have some concern that is preoccupying my thoughts? If so, try not to think about it for these ten minutes.

It is important not to rush into your daily activities when you have finished the exercise.

Exercise two – the semi-supine position

When you have got used to this first exercise, you may like to try lying down in what is known as the semi-supine position. The word supine simply means lying flat on the ground facing upwards. The following procedure is very simple but can be extremely effective in making you aware of muscular tension and reducing stress levels. Many people have said to me when I first suggest this exercise that it seems too simple to be really effective. They have usually been suffering from stress for many years, have been to see doctors and specialists, and have tried a vast range of treatments, none of which has given any lasting relief.

It can also be helpful to those suffering from stress-related muscular tension in the form of backache, neck problems or headaches. In addition, it can help to align the spine and release undetected tension in the neck and shoulders. If it is to be effective it should be carried out for 15 minutes every day for at least three weeks

The semi-supine position is excellent for reducing stress levels.

as it may take this amount of time before you begin to feel the benefits. Do not worry, however, if you miss the odd day.

This exercise was formulated from the Alexander technique which is discussed in greater detail in Chapter Seven. When you first start doing this exercise, you may feel overwhelmed with thoughts of all the things you need to do, or have feelings of guilt, which can cause you to become restless or fidgety. This is very common, especially if you are under stress, but don't give up, as after a week or so you will start to feel the benefits. As your mind and body calm down, you will become more efficient and will get more done in the long run.

- Lie down on your back with two or three thin paperback books under your head.

- Place your hands gently on either side of your navel.

- Bring your feet up near your pelvis so your knees are bent and are pointing up to the ceiling.

- Your feet should be making even contact with the floor and both your feet and knees should be about shoulder-width apart.

- Keep your eyes open throughout the procedure, as this will help you to remain in a state of alertness as you release the unwanted tension.

- Start to give 'directions' as outlined below in order to release muscle tension.

The main aim of this exercise is to release unwanted muscular tension throughout the body. It is far easier to let go of tension in this position, because gravity is working on your body in a different way from when you are upright. As F. M. Alexander, founder of the technique, discovered, most of us pull our heads back habitually and unconsciously, so the reason for having the books behind your head is that they will begin to prevent this from happening. The height of the books needed under the head will vary from one person to another but the main thing is to make sure that your head is not tilting backwards on to the books. As a general rule, it is better to have too many books than too few, but make sure your head is not pushed so far forward that it feels uncomfortable, or that your breathing is restricted. When first trying the semi-supine position, you may like to place a thin piece of foam or towel on top of the books if that feels more comfortable. If you are still uncertain, it is probably best to use a pillow or cushion for the time being until you are able to see an Alexander technique teacher who can instruct you more accurately.

The reason you have your knees bent is so that you can more easily release tension in the lumbar region (lower back) and in time you may find that your back gradually flattens on to the floor.

Giving directions

Tension in the muscles usually shortens them and Alexander devised a unique system to reverse this process, called 'giving directions'. This involves using your mind to think of the muscles lengthening. If practised regularly, this can dramatically reduce excessive tension that may be present in your body. Although you can try giving these directions for yourself at home, it is easy for people to misunderstand them and start to *do* the directions rather than just *think* of them. If you wish to get the most benefit out of this exercise it is strongly recommended that you practise under the guidance of a trained Alexander technique teacher, as this will accelerate the process, could save you a great deal of time and will ensure that you are on the right track. The following directions are particularly helpful when you are lying in the semi-supine position:

- THINK OF FREEDOM IN YOUR NECK

  This helps to release the excessive tension that often exists in this area and which causes the head to be pulled back and down on to the spine, thus interfering with the natural balance of the head. Neck tension may be difficult to detect, because often we have become accustomed to the feeling of tension over a long period of time.

- THINK OF YOUR HEAD RELEASING AWAY FROM THE SPINE

This allows the spine to lengthen and helps to release tension throughout your body.

- THINK OF YOUR BACK LENGTHENING AND WIDENING ON TO THE FLOOR

Again, it is very important not to do anything to make this happen. You may feel great relief as your back tension releases.

- THINK OF YOUR ELBOWS RELEASING AWAY FROM ONE ANOTHER

This will encourage freedom in the wrist and elbow joints and help to release tension in and around the shoulders. Make sure there is some space between your elbows and ribcage.

- IMAGINE YOUR SHOULDERS WIDENING APART

This will release muscular tension in the upper part of the chest, which will improve your breathing. This direction is particularly helpful for anyone with rounded shoulders.

- THINK OF EACH SHOULDER RELEASING AWAY FROM THE OPPOSITE HIP

This direction can be very beneficial for releasing the shoulders backwards and for reducing tension around the ribcage and in the abdomen.

- THINK OF YOUR KNEES GOING UP TOWARDS THE CEILING

This will help to release any tension in your legs and around your pelvis. You may find it helpful to think of your knees being supported by imaginary strings which are attached to the ceiling.

- THINK OF YOUR TOES LENGTHENING AS THE SOLES OF YOUR FEET SPREAD OUT ON TO THE FLOOR

This will help you to release tension in your toes and feet.

These are just a few of the directions that will help you to release muscular tension. It is important to remember that you must not do anything to find the right position: you merely send thought messages to the areas. The process of releasing tension depends on you doing less and not increasing the tension by trying to make something happen.

It may take a few weeks or more before you feel comfortable with this new position. Initially, it may be a good idea to lie down in the semi-supine position for ten minutes each day and lengthen the time progressively until you have reached 20 minutes. If at any time you experience pain in your back or neck while lying down, do not persevere. Simply get up and try again another time.

Benefits of the semi-supine position

Benefits that can be gained by practising the semi-supine position are:

- Reduced muscular tension throughout the body
- A lengthened spine, giving better support
- Tension released around the ribcage, which improves breathing
- Improved circulation (the blood can flow better through muscles that are relaxed)
- A more effective digestive system
- Freeing of nerves that have become trapped due to over-tense muscles
- More room for the internal organs to function
- A reduction in physical stress
- More energy to cope with daily life.

Most people will find that these benefits will arise only if this exercise is done on a regular basis. Try to lie down halfway through your day; if this is not always practical, lie down as soon as you get home from work. You may find that you have an improved night's sleep if you lie in the semi-supine position just before going to bed, while other people feel that starting the day in this way suits them better as they are aware of the benefits throughout the day. If you feel uncomfortable lying down after a heavy meal, choose a different time of day. It is much harder to release tension if you are feeling cold or lying in a draught so make sure you are warm enough and, if necessary, place a blanket over yourself while you are lying down.

3

breathing

*'What lies behind us, and what lies
before us are tiny matters,
compared to what lies within us.'*
RALPH WALDO EMERSON

The mechanics of breathing

Breathing is the most fundamental action that we perform – without it
we cannot accomplish anything. When we are relaxed our breathing
should be gentle, unhurried and rhythmical; when we are under stress,
however, our breathing becomes rapid and shallow. By bringing
awareness to our breath, we can help it to slow down, deepen and
return to its natural state. We all know that breathing is essential to our
survival, yet most of us rarely give any thought to this amazing miracle
that takes place continually throughout our life. It is the ever-present
life force that quietly and consistently enables us to perform all our
actions. It was the first action we performed as we entered this world
and it will be the last before we die. The gentle presence of the breath
is common to every one of us and it is our very essence.

Breathing is controlled by reflex:

- As we exhale a vacuum is created in the lungs
  which 'pulls' the next breath of air effortlessly
  into our lungs.

- As the breath comes into our lungs it causes the
  diaphragm and other muscles to stretch which

puts pressure on them causing them to contract at the end of each inhalation.

So a cycle of breathing is completed without our conscious effort, yet many people interfere with this simple process, totally unaware that they are doing so.

Everyone knows that without breath we would die in a matter of minutes, yet how many of us stop to realise this fact? Most of us take breath for granted, but without each and every breath, we would not even exist. The life force within us automatically causes us to take a breath without any effort on our part – we do not even have to remember to breathe.

Just pause for a moment to become aware of that silent inhalation and exhalation of your breath that is with you in every moment. Try to realise the fact that, without it you would not be able to see the words on this page, feel the texture of the book in your hand, or hear the sound of the pages as they turn. Spend a moment to ponder upon the mysteries of your breath and see if you can get a sense of the force or energy that is continually drawing the air into and then pushing the air out of your lungs.

Stress and breathing

The way we breathe – deeply or shallowly, slowly or quickly, rhythmically or agitatedly – is a clear indicator to show the level of stress we are under. Natural efficient breathing is an integral part of a relaxed muscular system, calm emotions and a clear mind. Many people unconsciously interfere with the simple act of breathing. The habit of over-tensing the muscular system, because of stress, affects the efficient functioning of the ribcage, the lungs, and even the nasal passage, mouth and throat (trachea) through which the air passes. This tension can also produce a general 'collapsing' or slumping of the whole torso, which can result in a massive restriction in the lungs' capacity to take in air, causing shallow breathing. We then have to make a great deal more effort in order to take in enough air. In short, through excessive tension we can even make the effortless act of breathing hard work.

This extra exertion goes largely unnoticed because we have become accustomed to shallow and strained breathing over many years, and it now feels normal to us. The only time that we become aware of the harmful effects of shallow breathing is when we exert ourselves. When running for a bus or climbing a flight of stairs, we suddenly find ourselves fighting for breath.

In many cases this interference with our breathing can be traced to feelings of stress. In severe cases, it is possible to observe some adults unnecessarily raising and lowering their shoulders while inhaling and exhaling, while others fix the ribcage, hold their abdominal muscles rigid and then lift and collapse the chest in order just to breathe. By comparison, if you observe young children you will see how their abdomen and ribcage move rhythmically with each breath. The rest of the body remains in a state of relaxation while the air is taken in and expelled almost effortlessly.

If the body is unable to get enough oxygen due to interference with the respiratory mechanism, the breathing rate will increase, leading to a quicker, shallower type of respiration. Shallow breathing can also cause or exacerbate anxiety, worry, panic attacks and depression, and in turn all these conditions are likely to cause interference with the breathing mechanism, so a vicious cycle of poor breathing, anxiety and stress is set up. Learning to breathe deeply, evenly and in a relaxed manner can be a very effective way to relieve stress.

Improving breathing

As a way of improving breathing some people encourage 'deep breathing' without giving any thought to how this is achieved. While their aim may be sound in principle, this method may encourage people to tense up as they 'take a breath' with excessive force. People might try to increase their lung capacity by 'pulling in' or 'pushing out' their breath, but this only further tenses an already over-strained muscular system. Straining the muscles in this way can result in arching the back and lifting the chest which actually restricts the breathing even further, causing detrimental breathing patterns or ingraining the original breathing habits even more deeply. Improving breathing to reduce stress should, in fact, be a process of unlearning bad breathing habits by relaxing rather than tensing.

The first thing to do to improve your breathing is simply to become aware of the breath without trying to change it. Even just placing your attention on how you breathe may bring about an improvement. Take a moment to get yourself comfortable and begin to be aware of your breathing. Ask yourself the following questions:

- How fast is my breathing?

- How deeply do I breathe?

- Do my ribs move as I breathe, and if so, where?

- How much movement is there in the abdomen when I breathe?

- Do I feel any restriction in my breathing, and if so, where?

- Where is there most movement – abdomen, ribs or upper chest?

If you find that you are breathing fast or shallowly you might like to try the following ways to help you breathe more naturally.

Yoga and breathing

'When the breath wanders, the mind is unsteady,
but when the breath is still, so is the mind still.'
HATHA YOGA PRADIPIKA

Yoga can be very helpful for the relief of stress symptoms as it incorporates relaxation, exercise, conscious breathing and meditation. A more detailed description can be found on page 66. Awareness and breath control (pranayama) is an important part of hatha yoga and there are many breathing techniques. Two of the better known techniques are deep breathing and nostril breathing.

Deep breathing

1. Sit or lie in a comfortable position

2. Breathe into your upper chest or clavicular area

3. Hold your breath for two or three seconds

4. Breathe out

5. Repeat five or six times

then

6. Breathe into your ribcage and feel the ribs expanding

7. Hold your breath for four seconds

8. Breathe out

9. Again repeat five or six times

then

10. Breathe into your abdominal area so you feel the abdomen moving

11. Hold your breath for five or six seconds

12. Breathe out

13. Repeat as many times as you like.

NB Air does not actually travel down as far as the abdomen – it just feels like it.

Nostril breathing

1. Clear your nose

2. Place one finger on your left nostril and exert gentle, but firm pressure

3. Breathe in deeply through your right nostril for eight seconds so that you can feel your abdomen moving

4. Hold your breath for four seconds

5. Now release the pressure on your left nostril and place another finger on your right

6. Now breathe out through your left nostril for eight seconds

7. Hold your breath for four seconds

8. Now breathe in through your left nostril for eight seconds

9. Again hold your breath for four seconds

10. Now release the pressure on your right nostril and place another finger on your left nostril

11. Repeat ten times.

Different yoga teachers may vary the length of time you breathe in and out and hold your breath, but the aim of breath awareness and control is the same.

The Alexander technique and breathing

In my role as an Alexander technique teacher, I find that when people first come to see me they do not specifically complain of breathing problems, but their breathing is often very erratic, very shallow or too fast. They often have acquired the habit of not finishing one breath before they start the next one. This is a direct reflection of the rushed way they have been living their lives, and they will frequently say that they feel that there are never enough hours in a day. The stressful conditions that many people have to work and live under cause excessive muscular tension, which in turn restricts breathing, causing detrimental breathing habits which affect the physical body, their state of mind and their quality of life. Even after a few Alexander lessons I have often found that people's breathing has naturally become slower and deeper.

If someone panics in a situation that requires calm and collected thought, we often tell them to 'take a deep breath' as a way of calming down. In the same way, by applying consciousness to the action of breathing we can change our breathing patterns and transform the way we feel.

Whispered 'ah' technique

F. M. Alexander (see page 81) devised this next exercise to help to improve breathing. When he first devised his technique he was nicknamed 'the Breathing Man'. Alexander realised that, contrary to what many people think, it is the out-breath, rather than the in-breath, that determines the way we breathe.

The whispered 'ah' technique simply helps the fundamental process of breathing by re-educating people to breathe naturally. You can do this exercise while sitting, standing or lying.

- First allow your tongue to relax and let it rest on the floor of the mouth with the tip lightly touching your lower front teeth. This allows the passage of air to and from the lungs to be unrestricted.

- Make sure your lips and facial muscles are not tense. To assist in this, it may be helpful to think of something that makes you smile.

- Gently and without straining, let your lower jaw drop so that your mouth is open. If you allow gravity to do most of the work you will make sure that your head does not tilt backwards in the process.

- Whisper an 'ah' sound (as in the word 'father') as you breathe out, until you come to the natural end of the breath. It is important not to rush the procedure by forcing the air out too quickly or trying to empty the lungs by extending the 'ah' sound as long as possible.

- Gently close your lips and *allow* the air to come in through your nose and fill up your lungs.

- Repeat this procedure several times.

Be aware of your breath as it travels in through your nose, down your throat and into your lungs. Just being conscious of your breathing will bring about subtle changes of which you may not even be aware. It is important that you do not deliberately try to change the way you breathe and that you simply become aware of the inhalation and the exhalation, as this is enough to bring about a beneficial change.

Regular practice of the whispered 'ah' will help you to notice detrimental breathing habits and eventually enable you to develop a more efficient respiratory system.

At first it may be advisable to perform the whispered 'ah' in front of a mirror as this will give you some idea of whether or not you are carrying out the instructions correctly. In particular, many people think that they are allowing their jaw to drop when in reality they are only opening their mouth very slightly.

Enjoyment of breathing

Breathing can be one of life's pleasures. It can be enjoyable to feel the gentle breath coming into and then leaving your body. Being aware of your breathing can be a powerful way in which to eliminate the effects of stress, as it calms your entire system and allows you to return to the present moment.

By allowing your breathing to become more natural it will also become deeper. When this happens many people feel more invigorated with a renewed enthusiasm for life. With every breath comes another opportunity to throw away our stressful habits and start to make real choices in our lives. Through free choice we have the power to turn life into what we want it to be, rather than trying to fulfil other people's expectations.

I would like to finish this chapter with a quote from the famous Indian poet Rahbindranath Tagore:

*'The same stream of life that runs through my veins night and day
runs through the world and dances in rhythmic measures.*

*It is the same life that shouts in joy through the dust of the Earth
in numberless blades of grass
and breaks into tumultuous waves of leaves and flowers.*

*It is the same life that rocked in the ocean cradle of birth and of death,
in ebb and in flow.
I feel my limbs are made glorious by the touch of this world of life
and my pride is from life,
the throb of ages dancing in my blood this moment.'*

4

meditation and visualisation

'People travel to wonder at the heights of mountains, at the huge waves of the sea, at the long courses of rivers, at the vast compass of the ocean, at the circular motion of the stars; and yet they pass by themselves without wondering.'
SAINT AUGUSTINE

Every day we are subjected to an ever-increasing number of sensory stimuli; as a result our minds becomes over-active to a point where we are unable to switch off and many of us are unaware of just how much mental activity we are constantly engaged in. This continual mental over-activity is one of the root causes of stress. Two techniques for reducing stress which millions of people have found helpful are meditation and visualisation. It is frequently the case that a person who finds it hard to meditate can visualise without difficulty and vice versa. There is no point causing yourself unnecessary tension by trying to do what does not come naturally to you. Through meditation and visualisation we simply allow this mental activity to settle down, and as a result our minds become more peaceful, calm and focused. You may like to try some of the techniques outlined in the following pages on your own, alternatively, there are many meditation or visualisation groups you can attend if you prefer the support and company of others.

Meditation

Meditation is a technique, or practice, that involves focusing the mind on something to bring about peace, stillness and tranquillity. It usually entails concentrating on an object, such as a flower, candle, sound or word, or on the breath. With practice your mind becomes quieter and the number of random unwanted thoughts begins to lessen. When you first try to meditate you may find that your mind seems more over-active than ever. This is normal and is a part of the process of becoming aware of the trivial thoughts we all carry in our minds for much of the time. Meditation can help you to contact something within that is peaceful, calm, rejuvenating and meaningful. Whether one calls this 'something' God, love, soul, peace or silence is irrelevant. It is an experience that anyone can benefit from, regardless of their opinions or beliefs.

Everyone has meditated at one time or another, often without realising it. It can happen while watching a beautiful sunset, being mesmerised by the moon or stars on a clear night, or being captivated by a jet plane as it disappears into the horizon. Meditation is simply a practical way of focusing your mind on one thing, which allows all other thoughts to quieten down; a way of engaging the mind in contemplation and allowing awareness to heighten. If you have been reading this book for a while, then put it down to take a break, sit quietly for a few minutes and focus on one object and one object only – this is meditation.

Effects of meditation

Experiences during meditation can vary significantly from person to person and depending on the techniques used. In general, a person practising meditation on a daily basis can expect to feel:

- a more relaxed body
- an increased awareness
- a clearer mind
- a sense of peace.

The most common physiological effects of meditation are a reduction in blood pressure, a lower pulse-rate and a decrease in the metabolic rate. Meditation may also bring about a change in your opinions and attitudes about life. Although a great deal has been written about the beneficial effects of meditation, the best attitude is to have no expectations when practising it, because having a sense of expectation of the results is likely to create unnecessary anticipation.

When you first start to meditate it is not unusual to fail to attain an experience of peace or mental clarity. Initially very few people are able to concentrate properly, but with practice this becomes easier. When thoughts come – as they do with everyone – it is important that you do not entertain them, but just refocus on what you have chosen to meditate upon. What is generally considered important in meditation is that you practise regularly each day – and just try your best to concentrate during the practice. By meditating regularly you will acquire the ability to increase your awareness and calm your mind.

For some people, meditation is primarily a spiritual practice, and in some cases the meditation practice may be closely tied to the practice of a religion, such as Christianity, Hinduism or Buddhism. It is possible, however, to learn how to meditate without any spiritual beliefs.

Starting to meditate

First of all choose a time and a place which is free from disturbance. It is not productive to meditate when you have something else to do, or when you're pressed for time. It's better to set aside a period such as the early morning or in the evening after work, when you can really give your full attention to the practice. Some people like to practise as soon as they get up as this helps them to feel calm for the rest of the day, while others prefer the afternoon or evening as this enables them to wind down after a busy day – choose whichever suits you.

A quiet room with little in it to distract your mind is the ideal setting for meditation. Light and space will naturally make you feel calm and focused, while a cluttered and gloomy room will have the opposite effect. The length of time spent meditating is also important, particularly as most people's days are quite structured with routines – you might like to begin with 15 minutes or so. Practise sincerely, without being mechanical about your routine, and try to follow these simple guidelines:

- · It works best if it is done every day, preferably at the same time

- It works better if it is done before a meal rather than after

- If possible a place should be set aside for your meditation, which should be quiet, warm and uncluttered

- Whether on a chair or on the floor, you should sit with a straight, but relaxed back

- You should be comfortable.

Becoming mindful

Adopt a position that will help you keep your back straight without strain. A simple upright chair may be helpful, or you may wish to sit cross-legged on cushions. If you are familiar with yoga you may like to use one of the lotus postures, but most importantly you should feel comfortable. Meditating while in pain or uncomfortable is pointless – it is not an endurance test! If your chin is tilted very slightly down this will help you to release any tension in your neck and spine, but do not allow your head to loll forward as this can encourage drowsiness. Place your hands on your lap, palms upward, one gently resting on the other and take a few moments to get comfortable.

Analyse how you are feeling. Are you anticipating or feeling tense with thoughts or doubts about whether you are doing it right? If so, try to relax your body a little – this should help to calm your mind. You may find some thoughts drifting into your mind, such as reflections, daydreams and memories. Instead of following or struggling with these thoughts, just bring your attention back to your body.

Now move your attention systematically from the top of your head down over your whole body. Notice the different sensations such as warmth, numbness and sensitivity in the joints of each finger, the beat of your heart, the pulse in your wrist and the rise and fall of your breath. This gentle exploration is called mindfulness and is one of the primary tools of all types of meditation.

Contrary to popular belief, in order to meditate it is not essential to develop a deep concentration to the point of excluding everything external. The aim is to create a 'bubble' of stillness that enables you to notice the workings of your mind, and eventually brings it to a peaceful state. The whole process of gathering your attention, noticing the breath, noticing that the mind has wandered off, and re-establishing your attention helps you to develop consciousness,

During meditation, you can sit on a chair or on a cushion on the floor. Whichever position you choose, make sure you are comfortable.

peace and a deeper understanding of life. Don't be put off by apparent 'failure' – simply begin again. Continuing in this way allows your mind eventually to calm down and reduces stress.

Meditation techniques

By concentrating on a particular thing, our attention can be taken beyond our continual mundane thought activity. You may choose a technique that uses one of the following:

- a solid object – such as a crystal or a beautiful stone

- a candle flame

- a flower

- a mandala – a picture with a focal point in the centre

- a mantra – a sound that has a flowing, meditative quality and may be repeated out loud or inwardly – the most well known is 'Om'

- the breath.

There is no *right* meditation technique for everybody. Certain techniques work better for certain people – the important thing is to find what works for you.

Object meditation

The word mandala comes from the Sanskrit for circle and a mandala is a complex circular design intended to draw the eye inwards towards the centre.

- Sit upright in a chair or on the floor in front of a solid object such as a crystal, a beautiful stone, a candle, a flower or a mandala

- Feel completely relaxed, try not to move

- Focus on the object of your choice

- If other thoughts enter your mind simply refocus your attention on to the object

- Continue for ten minutes.

After this meditation it may be useful to spend a few moments pondering upon the miracle of sight and see if you can get a sense of what it is that looks out of your eyes.

Mantra or sound meditation

- Again sit in a chair or on the floor in an alert yet relaxed way

- Inhale for five to six seconds

- Exhale for the same time – it is important that you do not strain

- Repeat the whole breathing process five or six times

- On the next out breath say the word 'Om'. It should sound like 'oommmmmmmm' and last as long as possible without strain

- Continue for ten minutes.

After this meditation you might like to take a few moments to contemplate the wonder of life and the life force that is allowing you to make that sound.

Chanting the 'om' mantra can bring peace to the mind.

Breath meditation

- Again make yourself comfortable yet alert

- Simply become aware of your breath as you inhale and exhale

- Follow your breath as it flows in through your nose, down your wind-pipe, and fills your lungs

- Follow your breath as it leaves your lungs comes up through your throat area and out through your nose or mouth

- If you find it hard to concentrate you could use the sounds 'So' and 'Ham'. Whisper 'So' on the in breath and 'Ham' on the out breath.

- Do not strain or hold your breath

- Repeat the whole process for as long as you wish.

Your breath has a steady, relaxing and tranquillising quality if you don't force it. Your mind may wander, but keep patiently returning to the breath. After this meditation it may be useful to spend a few moments contemplating the mystery of your breath and see if you can get a sense of the force or energy that is continually drawing the air in and out of your lungs.

Walking meditation

Although many meditation exercises, such as the ones above are practised while sitting, walking is commonly alternated with a standing meditation. Apart from giving you different things to notice, it is a skilful way to energise the practice if the calming effect of sitting is making you feel sleepy. It can also relieve stiffness if you have been sitting still for some time, and in this way it enables you to retain a meditative concentration.

- Find some open land where you will not be disturbed, and measure off about 30 paces in length of fairly flat ground as your meditation path

- Stand at one end of the path, and focus your mind on the sensations in your body

- First, let your consciousness rest on the feeling of your body standing upright, with your arms hanging relaxed by your side

- Allow your eyes to gaze at a point about four metres in front of you at ground level, thus avoiding visual distraction

- Now, walk slowly and gently to the end of the path

- Stop

- Perceive any sensations in your body while standing and breathe deeply for two or three breaths

- Turn, and walk back again

- While walking, be aware of any physical sensations – feel your feet as they make contact with the ground.

Keep bringing your attention back to the sensation of your feet making contact with the ground, the spaces between each step, and your breath as it enters and leaves your body.

It is common for the mind to wander – if it does, do not get annoyed – just bring it back to the task at hand. In more confined spaces, alter the length of the path to suit what is available. Alternatively, in bad weather you can walk around the perimeter of the room, pausing after a few minutes to stand in silence.

Meditation in everyday life

With the practice of meditation, you may discover a space within you that will give you a different perspective on life. You will be able to stand back from your problems, from what you think you are and from what you think you have achieved in life so far. You will learn the ability to go to a still centre of awareness within yourself and gently to detach yourself from the erratic existence of modern life. Try to take this different perspective into your everyday actions, like housework, walking down the street or eating your food. Try to be aware in everything you do. You may start to see, hear and feel things that have always been present, but that you have never noticed before. Becoming the master of your mind, instead of your mind controlling you, will help to bring harmony into your life. Perhaps you may now like to meditate upon these words by Helen Keller:

'I who am blind can give one hint to those who can see – one admonition to those who would make full use of the gift of sight:

Use your eyes as if tomorrow you would be stricken blind and the same method can be applied to other senses. Hear the music of voices, the song of the birds, the mighty strains of an orchestra, as if you would be stricken deaf tomorrow. Touch each object you want to touch as if tomorrow your tactile sense would fail. Smell the perfume of flowers, taste with relish each morsel as if tomorrow you could never smell and taste again.

Make the most of every sense.'

Visualisation

'They can because they think they can.'
VIRGIL

There are two kinds of visualisation that may be helpful in the relief of stress – creative visualisation and guided visualisation.

Creative visualisation

Creative visualisation is a method of using your mind to manifest something in your life. Many people are very sceptical of this technique while others are adamant that it works. You will have to be your own judge of this. Creative visualisation is simply a technique that uses your imagination to create what you want in your life. There is nothing at all new or unusual about creative visualisation, it is your natural power of imagination – your basic creative energy which you use constantly, whether or not you are aware of it.

We often use the power of creative visualisation in a relatively unconscious way. Because of our own deep-rooted negative concepts, many of us automatically expect limited happiness, difficulties and money problems to be our fate in life, yet this does not have to be the case. It is common to see other people make life much more difficult for themselves than it really needs to be, but this is much harder to realise when it comes to ourselves. We all have unconscious belief systems that create and control our lives.

Creative visualisation is a way of using your natural creative imagination in a more conscious way to create what you truly want in life. You can visualise anything you want from a loving relationship or inner peace and harmony to a satisfying and rewarding job or great wealth. It is believed that you can have whatever your heart desires. It is common knowledge that before something is created, it must first exist in thought form. Before you can make a meal you first have to think of the ingredients; the thought of wanting to go on holiday always precedes the trip; the potter has some idea of the design of his bowl before he throws the clay and the builder cannot build a house without a plan. Ideas are the blueprint, they create images of the forms, which through action eventually manifest themselves on the physical plane.

Imagination enables us to create an idea, a mental picture or a feeling – when we use creative visualisation we are simply using that same power of imagination to consciously create a clear image, idea or feeling of something we wish to manifest. Then we continue to focus on the idea, feeling or picture regularly, giving it positive energy until it eventually becomes an objective reality.

Your goal may be on the physical, emotional, mental or spiritual level. Here are some of the more common visualisations:

- a new home

- a new job

- a satisfying relationship

- a calm and serene feeling.

Creative visualisation exercise

It is important to be careful what you ask for, as any visualisation should not harm yourself or anyone else. For example you might become seriously ill after asking to lose weight or have an accident because you asked to leave your job.

To begin your creative visualisation:

- Get yourself comfortable in a lying or sitting position

- Relax as much as you can

- Decide on a goal that you wish to achieve

- Close your eyes and spend a few minutes imagining your wish as though it had already been accomplished. Use your imagination to think of the situation in as much detail as possible

- Repeat this process for a few minutes every day for a number of weeks

- Trust in the process

- Be patient.

Finally, it is important to realise that it may take some time to achieve your goal and that you may have to take some practical steps – it is not just a matter of bringing something into your life by thought alone, but by thought and action combined. Perhaps these words of

W. H. Murray will inspire you to use creative visualisation to obtain something you want:

'Until one is committed there is hesitancy, the chance to draw back, always ineffectiveness. Concerning all acts of Initiative and Creation, there is one elementary truth, the ignorance of which kills countless ideas and splendid plans, that the moment one definitely commits oneself, then Providence moves too. All sorts of things occur to help one that would never have occurred. A whole stream of events issue from the decision, raising in one's favour all manner of unforeseen incidents and material assistance which no man could have dreamed would come his way.'

Guided visualisation

Guided visualisation is considered by some to be a form of meditation as it can help to bring on a meditative state. You may wonder what exactly is meant by the word 'visualise'. Does one actually 'see' a mental image when one's eyes are closed? When many people first try to visualise, they feel that nothing is happening. This is usually because they are simply hindering themselves by trying too hard. If you are one of these people you need to stop worrying, relax and accept what happens naturally for you.

Try not to get stuck on the phrase 'to visualise.' It is not necessary to see images mentally. Some people see very clear, sharp images immediately they close their eyes. Others don't really 'see' anything at all, but they do sense or feel something. Some people are more visual while others are more auditory or feeling orientated. Whatever you experience when you visualise is fine.

Guided visualisation exercises
This simple visualisation can help to get you started:

- Get yourself comfortable in a lying or sitting position and relax as much as you can

- Visualise your body filling up with a warm light

- Visualising the breath as having the colour blue or green may be helpful. On the out-breath, let go of the stress, worry or negativity that you feel and extend the sense of this release right through your body and mind

45

- If you are under stress you might also find it helpful to imagine that you are breathing in the qualities of patience, calmness and serenity

- With every breath consciously welcome in the life energy that is keeping you alive

- Realise that you are more important than the things that cause you to be stressed.

Another guided visualisation that you can try:

- Get yourself comfortable in a lying or sitting position

- Think of yourself walking along a country lane

- You notice a gate and you open it and proceed into a field. Notice what crop or grass is growing in the field

- Observe your feelings as you walk across the field and through an opening that leads into a wood or forest

- You look around at any animals present as well as the trees and flowers growing there

- You sit down for a while. Is it warm or cold? Dark or light? Again mentally note any feeling you may have

- After a time you get up and wander to the edge of the wood and you see a mountain in front of you

- You proceed up the mountain and notice what you see on the way

- When you get to the top of the mountain you stand for a time to enjoy the panoramic views

- Once again observe how you are feeling

- You then see a beautiful blue ocean and you start to descend towards it

- Notice if you see any people or wildlife on your way down

- You reach the sandy beach and you take your shoes and socks off and you walk along the shore. You feel the warm water gently lapping up to your feet

- Notice any sea-life in the water or along the shore

- You then lie down on the soft sand and close your eyes.

Notice also how you feel in the different places – if you feel one has a calming effect on you then use that image in subsequent visualisations. This visualisation can form all or part of a period of meditation; you can decide for yourself what is appropriate.

Benefits of meditation and visualisation

Meditation or visualisation can help you to calm the mind, relax and energise the body, and can encourage positive feeling of tranquillity, joy and peace. It can enhance concentration and clarity, and help you to regain control of your mind and a greater sense of choice in your life. It is an extremely effective antidote to the over-stimulation and stress of modern life. In short, if you feel as though you are wound up, meditation or visualisation can help you to unwind. It is surprising how beneficial even a short period of stillness each day can be. The simple act of standing back from life's endless rounds of activity can help to bring life back into perspective. You will also find that once you are focused and relaxed, rich insights will be free to enter your mind.

5

transforming your lifestyle and living environment

*'We must learn to awaken and keep ourselves awake, not by
mechanical aids, but by an infinite expectation of the dawn, which
does not forsake us in our soundest sleep.
I know of no more encouraging fact than the unquestionable ability of
man to elevate his life by a conscious endeavour. It is something to
be able to paint a particular picture, or to carve a statue, and so to
make a few objects beautiful, but it is far more glorious to carve and
paint the very atmosphere and medium through which we look,
which morally we can do.
To affect the quality of the day, that is the highest art.'*
HENRY DAVID THOREAU

Are you one of those people who leap out of bed in the morning
because you have left too little time to prepare yourself for the day;
then speed out the door only to return a few minutes later because
you forgot something; then rush around frantically all day long trying
to catch up until you finally collapse into bed at night completely
exhausted? If so, this chapter is for you.

Giving yourself time

First and foremost you will need to look at your relationship with time, because if there is one factor that is more responsible for stress than any other it is probably having too much to do in too little time. Society today is ruled by time and although we keep inventing technology that saves us time it seems that hardly anyone feels that they have enough of it.

As young children we live in a timeless world where, even though we may move quickly, our movements are unhurried. Our actions are flowing, balanced and graceful as we have no thought about the past or the future – we are just enjoying the moment. As we get older, however, most of us are actively encouraged by society to become goal-oriented and as a result we abandon a spontaneous and creative way of being, in order to become more efficient and productive. We find ourselves living in a dehumanised society where money and social status often come before human feeling or creativity. We are so rushed off our feet that we have no time to be conscious and we are getting to a stage where giving ourselves time to perform a task properly is considered to be a luxury rather than a necessity.

Many of us feel continually under pressure to meet one deadline after another until we reach a stage where we are unable to relax. Our muscles remain in a state of tension even while we are asleep and we feel restless when there is nothing to do. Whether at school or at work, we are all rushing from one thing to the next and as a result we miss our life completely. We drive though villages without any recollection of doing so; we eat our food so fast we do not taste it and we perform actions without any consciousness of how we performed them. We rarely question what the great hurry is and where we are rushing to. Having watches and clocks should be for our convenience, but instead we become a slave to time.

Two hundred years ago life was much simpler. Today our senses are bombarded from morning to night. Just walk or drive down a busy street in any town and observe how much noise and visual stimulation we have to cope with all the time. Yet we do this without giving it a second thought. No wonder we often feel tired after our nervous system has been under this excessive strain.

The faster we live our life the faster life goes by. It is an interesting thought that we now own cars that can accelerate from 0 to 60 in a matter of seconds, which are capable of reaching speeds in excess 100 mph; we can fly from London to New York in a few hours, but we rarely ask ourselves 'Where am I heading for, and why do I really need to get to my destination so quickly?' A sobering thought is that the ultimate place that all of us are heading for is six feet under and by rushing through our life we just might get there a little quicker!

Think for a moment about how you feel when you are running late for an appointment; do you feel calm, worried or anxious? Do you think ahead and take steps to notify the people involved? Do you ever think that the other person you are meeting might also be late? When you do become tense or stressed when you are late, have you ever asked yourself why? What will happen to you if you do arrive late for work or for a social engagement? Often the answer is 'nothing' – our feelings of anxiety or even fear stem from our school days when being late was a punishable offence. Only when we realise that our fearful response is no longer appropriate are we able to change it.

This old Irish saying may help to cast a new perspective on time:

'Take time in your work – it is the price of success.
Take time to meditate – it is the source of power.
Take time to play – it is the secret of perpetual youth.
Take time to read – it is the way to knowledge.
Take time to be friendly – it is the road to happiness.
Take time to laugh – it is the music of the soul.
Take time to love and be loved.'

Pausing before acting

A moment of pausing gives us an opportunity to act with greater consciousness, providing a chance to act in a way that is more appropriate to the situation, rather than unconsciously reacting with unnecessary muscular tension. Pausing helps to prevent stress, allows the body to remain in a state of freedom and gives us time to think clearly. As discussed in Chapter One, stressful situations cause our 'fear reflex' to be triggered, causing excessive muscular tension throughout the body. If we are under constant stress at work, school or at home eventually this tension becomes a habit that occurs even when we are not under pressure. This interference is present throughout the body, produces a lack of balance and causes the body to wear out before its time. Recently I came across this lovely extract written by Buddhist monk Thich Nhat Hanh about drinking tea:

*'You must be completely awake and in the present to enjoy tea.
Only in the awareness of the present can your hands feel the pleasant
warmth of the cup. Only in the present can you savour the aroma,
taste the sweetness, appreciate the delicacy. If you are ruminating
about the past or worrying about the future, you will completely miss
the experience of enjoying the cup of tea. You will look down at the
cup and the tea will be gone.*

*Life is exactly like that. If you are not fully in the present, you will look
around and it will be gone. You will have missed the feel, the aroma,
the delicacy and beauty of life. It will seem to be speeding past you.'*

Small children automatically pause before many of their movements
and they are not afraid to say 'no' to many of the demands that are
placed on them – in fact it is often their favourite word. Frequently you
see them deliberately pausing before answering questions or
performing actions. It is the same with adults who do not live under
stressful conditions. For example we often consider the African
women carrying water on their heads as walking with grace and poise,
but if you also notice how they move you will see that they are never
in a hurry. They do not have the same concept of time as many people
in Western society as very few of them even own a watch. We adults in
industrialised society, by contrast, often rush into situations without
thinking about the consequences, frequently making mistakes which
could have been avoided. We even become irritated when the people
in front of us in a queue or on the roads seem to be taking their time.
We are often so totally goal-orientated that we do not even see why it
important to consider our actions as long as the job gets done as fast
as possible. Unless we can learn how to pause before acting it is
unlikely that we will be able to reduce our stress levels.

Taking a moment to stop and think is not only helpful when
carrying out actions, but is also useful during arguments. If we are
able to pause and calmly put our point of view across, then we are
much more likely to be able to achieve our desired result than if we
react emotionally.

From time to time it is important to ask ourselves 'What is it I really
want to achieve in my life, and am I going in the right direction to
achieve it?'

In his best selling book *The Ascent of Man*, Dr Jacob Bronowski
indicated that it is of the utmost importance that we give ourselves
time to think and consider our actions. He wrote: 'We are nature's
unique experiment to make the rational intelligence prove sounder

than the reflex.' He then went on to say that the success or failure of this experiment depends on our ability to impose a delay between the stimulus and our response. In other words, unless we are able to learn consciously to think before acting, we may be heading for the extinction of our own species.

We are pressurised to do so many activities in a limited amount of time that even the thought of pausing for a moment or two in a busy day seems to be pure indulgence. As the pace of life increases, it actually becomes even more important to take your time when making decisions. Is it not strange to reflect that there is rarely enough time to do a job properly in the first place, but there is always enough time to go back and correct the mistakes? The fact is that there is as much time as we allow ourselves. Perhaps you might like to pause for a moment and consider this old saying:

'When God made time he made plenty of it.'

Without changing our belief systems about time there can be no change in our life and our habits will continue to prevail. Remember if we do what we have always done we will obviously get the same results that we have always got. Although many people say they want to change the way they live, subconsciously they probably also want their lives to remain the same.

Benefits of pausing before acting

- It helps you to prevent over-tensing of your muscles, allowing your natural reflexes to co-ordinate and balance your body with ease

- It gives you time to be aware of any stress you may be putting on any part of your body

- It helps you to be aware of stress-forming habits and allows you to change them if you so wish

- It gives you a chance to say 'no' to taking on projects that will put you under stress

- It can save you time, because you are less likely to make mistakes, which take time to correct

- It encourages deeper, calmer breathing patterns.

Organisation

There are many practical steps that you can take to give yourself more time. These are simple constructive habits with which you can turn your life around. They can save you hours of frustration. The key is to organise yourself more efficiently.

Interestingly, the word 'organise' comes from the word organ – an internal part of our physical body with a specific function. Each organ has its own priorities and these function together within a whole organism. Just think what would happen if our internal systems were disorganised – for instance digesting food became more important than breathing, or healing a cut became more crucial than the heart regulator. In a very short time there would be chaos. In the same way a disorganised lifestyle can lead to chaos which manifests itself in the form of stress. You can organise yourself far more efficiently by planning ahead, prioritising and clearing out the clutter from your life. Here are some easy tips that may help you, but please try not to implement them all at once – it will only make you stressed!

In the morning

- Make sure you have a good, reliable alarm clock (but not one that wakes you abruptly)

- Place your alarm clock out of reach so that you have to get out of bed to switch it off

- Get up 15 minutes earlier than usual

- Prepare as much as possible the night before, for example by setting the breakfast table

- Do not answer the phone if you are running late

- Do not switch on the television or allow the children to do so as this will only make you late

- Have an area in the house where you put everything you need to take with you for the day

- Leave at least ten minutes before you have to in order to allow time for heavy traffic

- Just before leaving the house, pause to make sure you have remembered everything.

At work

- Keep your desk free from clutter, and tidy it at least once a day

- Keep all the things you use regularly close at hand

- Have an 'in' tray, an 'out' tray and a 'going home' tray

- Spend the first 15 minutes of the day organising your thoughts

- Spend an hour every Monday arranging your week's schedule

- Allow an extra 30 minutes a day for unexpected problems

- Never try to do more in one day than is realistic

- Prioritise – then do the essential things first

- Do not take on any further commitments if you are already overloaded

- If you feel continually overloaded ask for help

- Learn to say 'no' – politely

- Do not defend or make excuses for your decision to say 'no'

- Get a good, easy-to-read diary

- During meetings have your objectives clearly defined and written down

- Keep meetings short and to the point – always be clear about when the meeting will end and then be sure you finish on time

- Spend some of the day without interruptions so that you can catch up with paperwork in peace

- Do not have information in your office that frequently needs to be accessed by others

- Have plenty of pens on your desk. If a pen does not work – throw it away

- If you are delayed – phone and let the person know

- If you have to break an appointment, don't do it at the last minute. Most people do not mind rescheduling appointments if they know at least 24 hours in advance

- If you are running late – calm down. Nothing is more important than your health

- Spend at least 20 minutes at the end of each day reviewing the day's achievements and preparing for the next day

- Congratulate yourself and your work colleagues on your achievements.

At home

- Keep the house tidy

- If you are very busy get a cleaner

- Remove your shoes at the door – your carpets remain cleaner!

- Have a waste-paper bin in each room

- Immediately remove from your house what you do not need

- Once a month get rid of the clutter – the less you have the easier it is to keep the house clean

- Keep all work surfaces clear

- Have clear easy-to-read notice boards, calendars and shopping lists

- Once a year throw out all the clothes you have not worn that year

- Wash up after a meal or put the plates straight into the dishwasher

- Get a good can-opener that is easy to use

- Keep meal times sacred – no television. Take a tip from the French – take plenty of time to enjoy the food and the company

- Don't answer the phone just before or at meal-times – the person will ring back

- Switch on the answering-machine and switch off your mobile phone when you do not wish to be disturbed

- Only watch television programmes that you really want to watch. Don't forget that all televisions have an off switch

- If you work from home make sure you have two lines and do not answer the business line outside office hours

- Do the housework you hate most first

- Get the children into the habit of helping you as soon as possible

- Always clear up after one job before you move on to the next

- Put tools away when you have finished with them

- Have three laundry baskets – one for whites, one for coloureds and one for wool or delicate clothes.

Remember:

Proper

Pre-planning

Prevents

Poor and

Panicky

Performance.

You may be doing some of these things already, but you might like to try putting one or two of the others into operation each week to see which of them works for you. Don't forget that these suggestions are there to help, not hinder you.

Improving your surroundings

You can also reduce your stress levels by living in a harmonious environment. You may like to consider the following:

- Colour
- Lighting
- Space
- Noise
- Feng shui.

Colour

Many people believe that colour has a considerable effect on our moods. When we walk into a room our feelings can be affected by the colour scheme that we see. If we are living or working in a home or an office that is painted in an unsuitable colour it may be adding to our stress without us realising it. As you can see from the following suggestions having a blue or green room with living plants may be helpful in reducing stress. Of course there are many shades of the same colour, but as a rule different colours are thought to affect us in the following ways:

Red
This is a stimulating colour that can excite or awaken us. It is the colour of the early morning sun – and of many sports cars. It can be a good colour for children or those suffering from depression, but as a rule is not beneficial for those suffering from stress as it agitates the body's systems.

Orange

This is the colour for food and digestion as it is thought to stimulate the gastric juices. You will often find restaurants and kitchens are decorated in orange. Again this is not a good colour to use in a stressful environment.

Yellow

This is another stimulating colour as it is said to stimulate the intellectual mind. It is an excellent colour for schools, colleges or universities but not for reducing stress levels.

Green

This is one of the best colours, since it enhances relaxation and harmony. The 'living' green of plants and trees is the most effective, as it is calming on the eyes and encourages rest and relaxation. This is one of the reasons why a walk in a wood on a sunny day can be such a relaxing activity.

Blue

This colour can help you withdraw from the world and brings feelings of peace. It can help you to feel nurtured on a deep level and therefore it can be effective in reducing stress.

Violet

This colour helps you to be more alert and may even enable you to be spiritually receptive.

Lighting

During the day make as much use as possible of natural light, as this is the most beneficial for your eyes. Try to avoid fluorescent lighting as this can cause eyestrain or tension headaches. Have your desk at work near the window so that you can make the most use of natural daylight. At night try to use soft lighting or candles where possible as this can enhance a feeling of calm. At least once a month have an evening of candlelight or firelight only. You will be surprised at how different you will feel by the end of the evening.

Space

Not having enough space is another huge factor when it comes to stress. If you have a feeling of being hemmed in because of too much clutter, get rid of it, as this may be a prime cause of your stress. If possible live in a house or flat that is spacious, airy and light. Keep surfaces clear and put things away out of sight in cupboards where possible. Mirrors can also be useful to give you a sense of spaciousness if you have to live in a small space. If you have the space have a 'sorting out' room where you can put laundry, ironing and anything else that needs sorting out. Feeling crowded out by your possessions is bound to make you feel stressed and it is harder for you to find the things you need.

Noise

Noise is another major cause of stress. Most of the time you are probably completely oblivious to how much noise you are actually hearing, especially if you live in a city. Next time you are out for a walk, just try listening to how much sound there is around. Try to make a habit of turning off the television, radio or hi-fi when no one is paying attention to them or during meal-times. If you live on a busy street make sure you have double-glazing and keep the windows that open on to the road shut; have the rear windows open instead. Spend some time each day away from any noise.

You might also like to collect a few relaxing CDs or tapes that you can play at the end of a stressful day. In fact, an evening of candlelight with some beautiful music playing softly in the background can relax practically anyone.

Feng shui

Some feng shui tips might help you to create a harmonious environment. Feng shui is the Japanese art of maximising the potential and creating harmony within your home and there is a wide range of books available on the subject. Feng shui involves:

- Choosing particular colours when decorating rooms
- Arranging the furniture harmoniously
- Putting plants in certain places, particularly in corners of the room
- Using mirrors and crystals to enhance your home
- Removing clutter.

Improving your quality of life

Here are a few suggestions on how to make your life more enjoyable:

- Live more actively. Where possible – walk, don't ride
- Eat more slowly so that you can really taste your food
- Notice the animals and plants around you
- Start a garden – be as creative as you like
- Visit the woods, the sea or countryside – often
- Spend some quiet time each week in contemplation
- Listen to the birds sing
- Watch the seasons unfold
- Pick some apples and blackberries and make a pie
- Relax in a candlelit bubble-bath
- Trust your intuition
- Listen to your heart.

It is important to realise how affected we are by our environment. Making a few of the simple changes that have been suggested in this chapter can make a real difference to stress levels. Making these changes can be part of the process of beginning to take more care of ourselves, something so often forgotten in the rush and stress of modern life. Simply by improving our organisation skills and learning to pause before we act, we can generate a feeling of control and choice in our life.

6

physical exercise

*'The true miracle is not to fly in the air,
or to walk on water,
but to walk on this earth.'*
CHINESE PROVERB

Taking exercise

Due to increasing time pressures, one of the first things that we forget
to do when stressed is to exercise. Walking for just 20 minutes a day
can help to reduce stress dramatically and those who exercise
regularly will tell you they feel more energetic, happier and healthier.

Whilst it has been proven that physically active people have lower
rates of anxiety and depression than sedentary people, little scientific
work so far has focused on why this should be. To determine how
exercise might bring about such mental health benefits, some
researchers are now looking at possible links between exercise and
the brain chemicals associated with stress, anxiety and depression.
Preliminary results indicate that exercise improves the efficiency of
the body's physiological systems and its ability to respond to a variety
of stressful stimuli. It forces these systems, which are involved in the
stress response, to communicate much more closely than usual. It is
thought that a person who leads a sedentary life is less able to
respond effectively to stressful situations.

How does exercise reduce stress?

- Exercise can help reduce anxiety. Doctors now commonly recommend exercise to help treat nervous tension. Scientists have measured a decrease in the electrical activity of tensed muscles, which may be why people often report feeling less jittery and hyperactive after an exercise session.

- Exercise can relax you. The post-exercise 'euphoria' or 'endorphin response' improves your mood and leaves you relaxed.

- Exercise can calm you. This is due to the reduction of adrenaline which can build up in your body while under stress.

- Exercise can make you feel better about yourself. Being physically active stimulates feelings of self-worth, which contribute to stress relief.

- Exercise can improve your appetite. People who exercise regularly tend to eat more nutritious food. And it's no secret that good nutrition helps your body manage stress better.

- Exercise can remove toxins. Movement in our muscles can help the respiratory, digestive, skeletal and circulatory systems to work more efficiently allowing toxins in the body to be eliminated more effectively.

Exercise and your environment

So many people today cram their exercise into a short time period and into enclosed spaces – this can just add to the stress! Outdoors and away from the office is the best place to find a stress-free environment. Make sure that you give yourself enough time to exercise without rushing.

If you do attend exercise classes, try to avoid the overcrowded ones. If you do your exercises surrounded by people in a large class you will not get much individual attention and may well become discouraged as you see others doing certain exercises better than you do. This can be harmful as it encourages you to strain to keep up with them. Whichever exercise you choose, it is important to respect any physical limitations that you may have. Solo exercise may be more relaxing – a lot depends on your personality and what causes you stress. The main thing is that you enjoy your chosen form of exercise.

Some of the most enjoyable ways of exercising are also the simplest, such as:

- Walking

- Running

- Swimming

- Cycling.

It is also important that you exercise regularly as part of your everyday life. If possible, cycle or walk to work, and take the stairs instead of using a lift. Go swimming with family or friends to help to make it a social occasion, and go dancing!

Many exercises require participants to be blindly obedient to their instructor. These prescribed forms of exercise can increase muscular tension, adding to the stress. When choosing a specific exercise program you might like to consider one of the following methods, as these are much gentler and require more awareness of the body than many other forms of exercise:

- The Feldenkrais method

- Hatha yoga

- T'ai Chi

- Qi Gong.

The Feldenkrais method

'Each one of us speaks, moves and feels in a different way, each
according to the image of himself that he has built up over the years.
In order to change our mode of action we must change the image of
ourselves that we carry within us.'
MOSHE FELDENKRAIS

What is the Feldenkrais method?

The Feldenkrais method is a series of gentle movements that allows you
to increase your ease and range of motion and improve your flexibility
and co-ordination. This method can be beneficial at any time of life,
regardless of your age or physical condition. The practitioner verbally
or with 'hands on' guides you through a sequence of movements,
which can be done while lying on the floor, standing or sitting on a
chair. These movements can help you to discover how you perform
each action and perhaps work out a more efficient way to move.

You learn to relax as well as becoming aware of and eliminating
unconscious habitual patterns of movement.

History of the Feldenkrais method

The originator of the Feldenkrais method, Dr Moshe Feldenkrais was
born on the Russian–Polish border in 1904. At the age of 13 he left
home and travelled on foot for a year until he reached Palestine
where he worked as a labourer, cartographer and tutor in
mathematics. He also became active in gymnastics, soccer and then
in the martial art of Ju-Jitsu. During his mid-twenties he left for France
and eventually became a graduate of *l'Ecole des Travaux Publiques de
Paris*, in Mechanical and Electrical Engineering. Later he earned his
Doctorate of Science in Physics from the Sorbonne in Paris where he
assisted Nobel Prize winner Joliot-Curie in early nuclear research.

While in Paris Feldenkrais also studied with Jigaro Kano, the
creator of modern Judo, and during 1936 Feldenkrais became one of
the first Europeans to earn a Black Belt in Judo. He then started to
introduce Judo in the West through teaching and books. During the
Second World War, he patented a number of sonar devices while
working in anti-submarine warfare for the British Admiralty.

After crippling knee injuries incurred as the result of a soccer
injury, Feldenkrais called on his background of mechanical

engineering and the martial arts and taught himself to walk again. In the process he developed an extraordinary system for accessing the power of the central nervous system to improve human functioning.

Feldenkrais studied intensively in psychology, neuro-physiology and other health-related disciplines, and in 1949 he returned to Israel where he continued to integrate and refine his ideas into the system we know today as the Feldenkrais method.

How does the Feldenkrais method work?

There are two aspects of learning that are basic to the Feldenkrais method: 'awareness through movement' and 'functional integration'.

Awareness through movement

In much the same way as yoga, 'awareness through movement' is usually taught in a group situation. You wear loose, comfortable clothing and are guided through a series of simple movements, which are similar to the movements you make every day. The Feldenkrais teacher will show you many different ways that you can do the same movement and you will explore these until you discover which is the best for you. In the process of learning Feldenkrais you will start to move your body with greater ease.

During these classes you improve at your own rate – there is no pressure to achieve. While performing these simple movements you will learn to listen to your body and leave behind detrimental habitual patterns of movement. You will develop new ways of performing simple

'Awareness through movement' classes help you to listen to your body and leave behind detrimental patterns of movement.

actions. After these lessons people may feel taller or lighter, breathe more freely, and find that their physical discomforts have eased. Eventually, these new movements become part of everyday living.

Functional integration

The most direct way to experience Feldenkrais is through 'functional integration'. This is a hands-on kinaesthetic communication, which is done on a one-to-one basis. Again wearing loose, comfortable clothing, you sit or lie on a low, padded table. The practitioner guides you through a series of precise movements that release muscle tension. Through this primarily non-verbal technique the Feldenkrais practitioner is able to sense how far a person can move, and what is needed in each movement for a person to become as flexible as possible. The practitioner communicates this technique with his or her hands using gentle touch. These movements can help you to alter old habitual patterns which no longer serve you, and provide new information to the nervous and muscular systems. Functional integration can be useful for anyone who needs to give attention to particular discomforts as well as those who simply want to feel better physically and mentally.

Although both ways take the form of specific exercises, they are really sequences of movement specially designed to develop your sensitivity, and increase your vitality by awakening unused areas of body. While you are rediscovering the flexibility and full use of the body you will gain nothing by forceful pulling. This is why people learning the Feldenkrais method are strongly urged to take their time and to think through the exercises as they are doing them.

Hatha yoga

'The self is not the individual body or mind, but rather that aspect deep inside each individual person that knows the truth.'
SWAMI VISHNU DEVANANDA

What is hatha yoga?

Hatha yoga is the practice of a sequence of physical postures with a special emphasis on breathing. It helps to release tension and promote strength and flexibility of body, mind and emotions. The breath is the key in hatha yoga, and when done correctly every movement or posture is fully co-ordinated with the breath. This continual concentration on inhalation and exhalation helps to focus the mind, and allows one to reach a quiet, still place inside. From that quiet place, the effects of holding each posture can be observed.

All yoga postures should be easy to hold without strain.

Hatha yoga consists of specific yoga postures which are the result of a thousand years of experience. Postures are usually named after certain images such as plants (the tree or the lotus), birds (peacock), animals (cat or cobra), or even humans (poise of a child) and reflect the physical or psychological effects of these postures. For instance, the cobra or cat poses makes the spine flexible while the poise of a child pose helps the body to conserve energy.

Yoga postures should not be confused with mere exercise, which only helps to strengthen and develop muscles. Essentially yoga helps you to prepare the body so that the mind can practise meditation more or less without obstacles. These positions of the body can strengthen, purify and balance the endocrine, nervous and circulatory systems. While yoga postures are rarely prescribed to treat illnesses, they do have therapeutic effects and can help to reduce stress and prevent illness.

Everyone, regardless of age or fitness level can practise hatha yoga. You don't have to be flexible to begin, and there is no particular philosophy or religious belief that you must hold in order to feel the benefits. Yoga is extremely adaptable and is beneficial to anyone who wishes to increase their vitality and sense of well-being. Just make sure that you choose a teacher who is right for you and never push yourself too far – the flexibility of your body will increase in time.

History of hatha yoga

Yoga is often thought of as consisting only of physical postures, but this is only a small part of what yoga involves. The word yoga means 'union' – the union of the human soul with the Universal Soul. Although yoga is a product of Indian civilisation and has been influenced by its religions, it is in fact a practical spiritual science that does not belong to any particular religion. It brings positive results which are independent of religious orientation. Yoga goes so far back into the untold history of India that it is impossible to know its origins. It has always been and still is being refined and improved.

Through specific teachings yoga enables you to cultivate a balanced mind, calm emotions and a fit and flexible body. Most yoga teachings state that the human body is a temple of the Spirit and, as such, should be carefully maintained. The original aim of hatha yoga was to prepare the body for the spiritual path by performing physical and breathing exercises.

Benefits of hatha yoga

Yoga postures, breathing and relaxation can alleviate many common problems that leave you feeling tired and drained of energy. The ultimate benefit of yoga is the awakening of a deeper awareness and understanding of the life energy within you. This begins with an increase in physical awareness. As you develop the ability to synchronise your breathing with certain movements, your attention begins to turn inward and you eventually develop the ability to stay calm during stressful situations.

Practising physical yoga is not difficult. Yoga postures should be easy to hold comfortably. Regular practice will help you to move your body through the full range of movements. Postures consists of forward and backward stretches, twists and lateral stretches, which are designed to lengthen and strengthen all of the muscle groups. The combination of slow, prolonged stretching and the holding of postures helps to release tension from your muscles. As a result, a new flexibility and strength, an improved alignment, and an expanded range of motion is achieved. Special attention is given to the shoulders, neck, back and abdomen because these tend to be areas of weakness and tension for most adults. You may also notice an improvement in your breathing, resulting from the release of tension in the muscles of your chest and upper back.

Regular practice, while helping you to relax and increasing your self confidence, can also facilitate other lifestyle changes, such as eating a more wholesome diet and modifying the use of drugs, alcohol and tobacco.

Most yoga classes end with a period of rest and relaxation. During this relaxation your breathing rate, pulse and blood pressure decrease and muscles tension is reduced. This promotes a healthy balance of hormones. Eventually, many of these effects will be sustained outside practice time.

T'ai Chi

'Knowing others is intelligence;
Knowing yourself is true wisdom.
Mastering others is strength;
Mastering yourself is true power.'
LAO-TZU

What is T'ai Chi?

T'ai Chi can perhaps best be thought of as a moving form of meditation and with Qi Gong is the physical exercise aspect of Traditional Chinese Medicine. The Chinese characters for T'ai Chi can be translated as 'supreme force'. The idea that there is a vital force flowing around the body is very common in Chinese philosophy. Any impediment of this flow is believed to bring ill-health to the body and by using T'ai Chi exercises you can help to restore the balance of this 'chi' and enhance your health and vitality. 'Chi' circulates along paths through the body called meridians. These are closely related to the nervous and vascular systems and correlate closely with the principles of acupuncture and shiatsu (see Chapter Seven).

There are a number of 'forms', or sequences of movement in T'ai Chi which were originally derived from the natural movements of animals and birds. T'ai Chi is performed in a slow, soft and graceful way with smooth transitions from one posture to another. Although T'ai Chi has become a martial art many practitioners emphasise the meditative rather than the combative aspects of this art.

Another important aim of T'ai Chi is to calm the mind by focusing precisely on mastering these 'forms'. This provides a practical

T'ai Chi is thought to be derived from the natural movements of animals or birds.

channel for learning about such things as balance, alignment and rhythm of movement. Many people who practise T'ai Chi claim that they are able to stand, walk, run and move with greater freedom and are able to correct poor postural alignment or harmful movement patterns which can contribute to tension or injury. T'ai Chi has a calming and relaxing influence on body, mind and emotions.

History of T'ai Chi

Like yoga the origins of T'ai Chi are lost in ancient history. It is one of a variety of movement systems originating in China, which are associated with health and peacefulness. T'ai Chi has always been seen as contributing to a purposeful and productive life which can help to develop wisdom and bring out a person's latent potential.

T'ai Chi was born out of the very origins of Taoism and the movements are reflected in the writings of Lao-tzu:

'Yield and overcome;
Bend and be straight.
He who stands on tiptoe is not steady.
He who strides cannot maintain the pace.'

It is thought that one of the earliest forms of T'ai Chi took place around AD 230, when a physician called Hua-tuo taught that the body needed to be regularly exercised to help with digestion and circulation. He believed health and longevity could be achieved by specific exercise combined with herbal medicine, and taught the movements that imitated the following five creatures: the tiger, deer, bear, ape and bird. He helped to design a system that duplicated the movements of these animals to help exercise every joint and muscle in the body.

During the sixth century T'ai Chi was taken up by monks who were in poor physical condition as a result of too much sitting meditation and not enough exercise. They started to incorporate T'ai Chi into their daily routine.

Throughout the ages T'ai Chi has been developed by various masters. We now have many different forms, named after those who devised them. During the twentieth century the Chinese government became worried that many people in China were becoming unhealthy and that they would, therefore, have to pay out vast sums of money in health care. To deal with the problem they made T'ai Chi mandatory throughout the country and anyone travelling through China was amazed to see large groups of people in public parks performing this flowing exercise.

Styles and forms of T'ai Chi

Most of the different schools or styles of T'ai Chi have been given the family name of their founders. The principal schools of T'ai Chi that are in existence today are: Chen Style, Hao or Wu Shi Style, Hu Lei Style, Sun Style, Wu Style, Yang Style and Zhao Bao Style. Unless you have been recommended one in particular it is a good idea to try several of them and find the one that suits you best.

In each style of T'ai Chi there are 'long forms' which are traditionally considered to consist of 108 movements and help to develop the basic principles of T'ai Chi:

- Balance

- Calmness

- Alignment

- Awareness

- Internal stillness

- Performance of smooth movement rhythms.

The popular 'short forms', which have been developed more recently, are simply a more concise version of the original long form.

Benefits of T'ai Chi

As well as being a physically beneficial exercise T'ai Chi promotes personal growth. This occurs on many levels as it can help you to be a more conscious person and to bring out qualities of gentleness and caring that many people keep hidden. Some say that this is because it helps to strip away the armouring that is developed in childhood and allows a more relaxed being to emerge.

T'ai Chi is a mixture of harmony and opposites. As you practise you may feel:

- Energised, yet calm

- Animated, yet relaxed

- Yielding, yet powerful

- Moving, yet still.

These are just a few of the opposites which occur simultaneously while practising T'ai Chi and for those people who are used to a conventional way of exercising it can be an interesting procedure as it challenges your preconceived way of using your body.

Qi Gong

'The snow goose need not bathe to make itself white.
Neither need you do anything but be yourself.'
LAO-TZU

What is Qi Gong?

Qi Gong is practised by millions of people in China and is associated with a broad range of mental and physical exercises generally regarded as beneficial to health maintenance and health improvement. Qi Gong is the art and practice of internal energy development, and works mainly on the bodily fluids – the blood, the lymph, synovial and cerebro-spinal fluids – to strengthen the body. As with T'ai Chi, it is also related to the martial arts. Qi Gong, or Chi Gung as it is sometimes written, is a self-healing art that combines movement and meditation, and can be sometimes be thought of as the skill of attracting vital energy. Qi Gong (pronounced 'chee gung') comes from two Chinese words: 'Qi' or 'Chi' meaning energy or life force, and 'Gong' or 'Kung' meaning a skill or a practice. Qi Gong therefore means a skill or practice of cultivating energy.

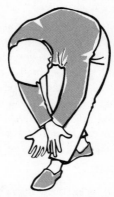

The simple, powerful exercises of Qi Gong combine breathing, movement and visualisation.

There are various kinds of Qi Gong which are broadly categorised as internal and external. Internal Qi Gong is much like meditation, using visualisations to guide the energy, while external Qi Gong includes movement accompanying the meditation. Visualisation techniques are employed to enhance the mind–body link and to assist healing. Like yoga, both kinds of Qi Gong focus on breathing. Qi Gong is also a part of Traditional Chinese Medicine and has many similarities and links with T'ai Chi.

History of Qi Gong

Many existing forms of Qi Gong are related to Chinese Traditional Qi Gong which is thought to be about 7000 years old. Long before the establishment of modern day religions, people realised that body movement, mental concentration and various ways of breathing could help them regulate certain functions of the body. Due to their simple lifestyle and close contact with nature, these people were more aware of the vital life force which they called 'Chi'. During this time Qi Gong was widely used for health preservation, disease prevention and the treatment of illnesses. It was even used to develop special spiritual or physical abilities.

From about 500 BC the popular practice of Qi Gong declined as official suppression drove many great Qi Gong masters into seclusion in the mountains. After over two thousand years Qi Gong began to re-emerge in modern society and in the late 1970s, and after many debates and public demonstrations in China, it became recognised once again in Chinese society.

A number of accomplished Qi Gong practitioners started publicly treating patients and teaching Qi Gong and also started to work together with scientists to provide a scientific foundation for Qi Gong. Over 200 popular Qi Gong practice methods are available and it is thought that over 60 million people are practising Qi Gong in one form or another. Qi Gong healing is now an officially recognised medical treatment in China and an increasing number of people are coming into contact with it throughout the world.

Benefits of Qi Gong

Physical and mental health are closely linked through the mind–body connection and Qi Gong can help to improve both aspects of your life. It combines all the benefits of meditation such as the ability to reduce stress, lower blood pressure and develop awareness, with those of physical exercise. It can also increase your ability to detect where your body needs changes related to diet, exercise, sleep and lifestyle.

This mind–body connection is an all important issue as it can influence the course of many chronic diseases. In China, Qi Gong gained recent fame in the treatment of cancer, but Qi Gong has long been famous throughout China for curing a wide range of chronic diseases and promoting health.

Chinese Traditional Qi Gong is a technique for the cultivation of mind and body for the betterment of character and destiny. By cultivating the mind and body, one can change one's innate character for the better, gain a clear perspective of life in relation to this world, and even help to realise the purpose of life. In short, Qi Gong can help you to live a healthier and happier, more productive and longer life.

7

alternative therapies

*'The cure of the part should not be attempted
without the treatment of the whole.'*
PLATO

Although the therapies in this chapter are commonly described as alternative, several of them have been around for thousands of years and, in fact, predate the methods that are mainstream today. Interest in these methods of healing has increased dramatically in recent years as more and more people are looking for an approach that encompasses their mind, body and emotions. This new kind of patient requires not only to be nurtured, but also to be empowered, treated with respect and made a partner in the healing process.

As the benefits of these treatments are being reported in the scientific literature, the degree of acceptance and acknowledgement from the conventional medical establishment is growing. There is even a recent trend for medical schools and hospitals to invite alternative therapists to lecture or to develop programmes in the schools to complement their more conventional curricula.

These therapies have not only been proven to cure problems and deal effectively with stress, but can also be used as preventative measures to keep the body healthy and less prone to disease. It is important to realise, however, that everybody responds to treatment in a different way, so take your time to choose the one that works best for you. The therapies covered in this chapter are: Acupuncture, Alexander technique, Aromatherapy, Chiropractic, Hypnotherapy, Osteopathy, Reflexology and Shiatsu.

Acupuncture

'Life is a series of natural changes.
Do not resist them – that only creates sorrow.
Let reality be reality.
Let things flow naturally forward in whatever way they like.'
LAO-TZU

What is acupuncture?

Acupuncture is an ancient art that originated in the Orient. It consists of inserting fine needles into the skin to correct imbalance or disharmony within the body. The needles are inserted along specific channels, known as meridians, in order to allow energy to flow freely along these pathways. Different conditions require different meridians and acupuncture points to be used.

History of acupuncture

It is believed that acupuncture has been used for over 3000 years, but only recently has it become the most widely used alternative therapy in the West. Not much is known about its actual origin, but it is thought that Chinese doctors started to develop acupuncture after they observed physical and mental changes in their warriors who had been stabbed or speared in battle. In the early days, around 1500 BC, 'stone probes' were used to adjust the flow of energy and it was not until much later that needles were found to be more effective. Acupuncture has always been a major part of Traditional Chinese Medicine which also includes Chinese herbal remedies, diet, massage and exercises such as T'ai Chi and Qi Gong.

Although many scientists today still do not understand why acupuncture works, they acknowledge that the treatment is effective. Many medical practitioners, physiotherapists and chiropractors now use acupuncture in conjunction with their own therapy to combat pain as well as to cure and prevent illness. In 1980 acupuncture became more accepted in the West when the World Health Organisation released a list of 43 illnesses that can be effectively treated with acupuncture.

How does acupuncture work?

The Chinese have a unique system of categorising illnesses that is very different from its Western equivalent. To understand how acupuncture works, it is necessary to understand a few basic principles of Chinese medicine. The first principle is that of 'yin and yang'.

Yin and yang

Chinese medicine relates to the complementary but opposing forces of yin and yang.

Yin is considered to be the material of which all living things are made, and yang is the energy that sustains and operates all of life's functions. Yin and yang are two opposite and opposing forces – yin being the female, passive or receding aspect of nature and yang, in contrast, being the male, active or advancing aspect. Although yin and yang are two opposing forces, just like light and darkness they also depend on each other for their existence, and thus cannot be thought of separately. The balance of yin and yang is never motionless – it is always changing; each one is constantly transforming the other.

The four characteristics of yin and yang are:

- Yin and yang are opposite to each other
- Yin and yang are dependent on each other
- Yin and yang consume each other
- Yin and yang transform each other.

One of the most famous books about Chinese Medicine, *The Yellow Emperor's Classic of Internal Medicine* (AD 400) states that:

'To live in harmony with yin and yang will bring peace –
To live out of harmony with yin and yang will bring chaos.'

When people are under stress it is thought that they have too little yin or too much yang and that in order to reduce stress this imbalance needs to be redressed. The chart below shows the opposite qualities of yin and yang.

YIN	YANG
Female	Male
Dark	Light
Cold	Hot
Wet	Dry
Slow	Fast
Internal	External
Water	Fire
Moon	Sun
Passive	Active
Contraction	Expansion
Rest	Movement
Soft	Hard
Moon	Sun
Night	Day

Qi

Qi, Ki or Chi (pronounced 'chee' in China and 'key' in Japan) is the energy in all living things; the Chinese believe that this energy can be found in the tiniest particles of matter and is the building block of everything that has been created. We are only alive and moving because Qi moves through us. All things that we hear, see or feel are just different manifestations of Qi.

The Qi inside our body is created from a combination of the air we breathe and the food we eat. Anything that affects the flow of Qi will cause ill health. Qi moves through our whole body, but there are certain defined channels where the flow of Qi is more concentrated. These channels or pathways are known as meridians. When you are under stress Qi is unable to flow freely and this therefore upsets the yin/yang balance.

Meridians

There are 12 main meridians in the body along which Qi flows. The meridians form a continuous circuit of pathways, which allow the Qi to reach all parts of the body. Each meridian is named after a physical organ, but it is important to realise that each meridian does not merely relate to a particular organ, but rather to a particular function relating to each organ.

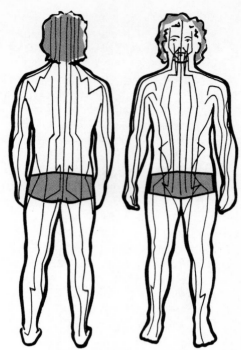

The acupuncture meridians.

MERIDIANS	FUNCTION
Lungs	Intake of air and vitality
Large intestine	Elimination
Stomach	Intake of nourishment
Spleen/Pancreas	Digestion and transformation
Heart	Balance of emotions
Small intestine	Assimilation
Bladder	Purification
Kidneys	Growth
Heart governor	Circulation
Triple heater	Protection
Gall bladder	Distribution
Liver	Detoxification

Visiting an acupuncturist

The acupuncturist will first ask you questions about your illness and lifestyle and will take many factors into consideration before treating you. He or she will also take your pulses, note your predominant mood and will often examine your tongue as well. By careful analysis of your whole being, the acupuncturist will prescribe a method to correct any imbalance. As with all other aspects of Chinese medicine, the object of acupuncture is to treat the whole person and not just the symptoms of the illness. Your illness is seen as the manifestation of an imbalance in your energy levels.

When the acupuncturist treats you he, or she, inserts hair-fine needles into specific acupuncture points on a meridian. This helps to stimulate the flow of your natural healing energy and brings the body's energy back to balance. You will usually only feel a slight sensation as the needle pricks the surface of your skin. The insertion of an acupuncture needle is not usually a painful experience. Sometimes patients will sit with eyes closed and teeth clenched anticipating the pain, and will often be surprised when they realise that the needles are already in place. The needles are usually left in place for 20 to 30 minutes and it is not unusual for a patient to fall asleep during a treatment.

To achieve the maximum effect it is sometimes necessary for the acupuncturist to cause a 'needling sensation'. This involves the needle being slightly turned while it is in the skin, and the sensation experienced by the patient will vary. It is this needling sensation that can sometimes be a little painful, and the sensation may also travel up or down the meridian that is being treated.

It is very difficult to predict how a patient will respond to acupuncture. Sometimes only one treatment is required, whilst another person may need a number of treatments to gain the same result for the same condition. In general most people do not respond immediately to one treatment, and a minimum of four to eight treatment sessions is usually required for the best results. Three treatments should be adequate to assess whether a patient will respond to acupuncture. If there has been no response to treatment after the first three sessions then it is doubtful whether any response will occur at all.

It is important to note that sometimes a patient may experience a temporary worsening of symptoms after treatment and that this can be seen as a good sign. Such 'reactions' only last for a short time, perhaps a day or two, and are usually then followed by improvement.

Acupuncture is not a self-help technique and you should always consult a trained acupuncturist – addresses may be found at the back of the book.

The Alexander technique

'It is essential that the people of civilisation should comprehend the value of their inheritance, that outcome of the long process of evolution which will enable them to govern the uses of their own physical mechanisms. By and through consciousness and the application of a reasoning intelligence, man may rise above the powers of all disease and physical disabilities. This triumph is not to be won in sleep, in trance, in submission, in paralysis, or in anaesthesia, but in a clear, open-eyed, reasoning, deliberate consciousness and apprehension of the wonderful potentialities possessed by mankind, the transcendent inheritance of a conscious mind.'

FREDERICK MATTHIAS ALEXANDER

What is the Alexander technique?

The Alexander technique is a method of self-awareness, a simple technique that can be understood by anyone, yet at the same time is very profound. It is a process of unlearning physical, mental and emotional habits that cause stress and replacing them with the conscious control of actions, thoughts and feelings; a way of becoming aware of and improving balance, posture and co-ordination by helping you to change the way that you move while performing everyday actions. This releases excessive muscular tension that has accumulated over years of stressful living and which is often the root cause of health problems. The human body is an amazing instrument, but due to the strain that many of us are under we subconsciously interfere with its natural working,which can lead to common ailments such as backache, headaches, poor breathing and other stress-related illnesses. The technique is not strictly speaking a therapy as it is something that you learn for yourself, but it can be very therapeutic.

History of the Alexander technique

Frederick Matthias Alexander was born on the North-west coast of Tasmania, Australia in 1869. He was a very sickly child, suffering from asthma and other respiratory problems. In his early twenties he gained a reputation as a first-class actor and reciter, and went on to form his own theatre company specialising in one-man Shakespeare recitals. As he became increasingly successful, his performances put more and more strain on his vocal cords. Within a short time the stress began to show, and his voice regularly became very hoarse during his performances. He approached various doctors and voice trainers who gave him medication and exercises, but nothing seemed to make any lasting difference. He became increasingly anxious as he realised that his entire career was in jeopardy.

Determined to find a solution, Alexander started to use a mirror to observe himself when reciting, in the hope that he would see what it was that he was doing wrong. He clearly saw that he had a habit of pulling his head back and downwards on to his spine with excessive muscle tension when he was reciting, and that this was causing a strain of the vocal cords. Until this point Alexander had been unaware of this habit and with further investigations he saw that his whole muscular system was being affected. Over the next few years Alexander devised a technique which not only solved his voice problem, but also cured his asthma and breathing problems.

When Alexander returned to the stage, many of his fellow actors sought his help. News spread, and doctors began referring their patients to Alexander. He had enormous success in treating various ailments using the gentle guidance of his hands, as well as verbal instructions.

In 1904 Alexander sailed to England in order to bring what he had learned to a wider audience. He set up a practice in central London, and worked there until his death in October 1955.

How does the Alexander technique work?

The technique eliminates stress and muscle tension in the body by teaching a person how consciously to choose a different reaction to stressful situations. Learning the technique consists of three stages:

1. Releasing unwanted tension that has accumulated over many years of standing, sitting or moving in an unco-ordinated manner.

2. Learning new ways of moving, standing or sitting that are easier, more efficient and put less stress on the body, thus reducing excessive wear on the bones and joints, and allowing the internal organs space to function naturally.

3. Learning new ways of reacting physically, emotionally and mentally to various situations.

The two main principles of the Alexander technique are called 'inhibition' and 'direction'.

Inhibition

In the Alexander technique inhibition means to inhibit any immediate response to an external stimulus. This simply means that a person pauses before reacting to certain situations in order to choose a different, less stressful way of responding. Inhibition is the fundamental key to the Alexander technique, for without it we do not have a chance to alter our stress levels. The dictionary definition of inhibition is: 'the restraint of direct expression of an instinct'. The word has more recently come to mean the suppression of feelings or the inability to be spontaneous, but this is mainly because the psychologist Sigmund Freud used the term in this particular context.

Directions

The process of 'giving directions' involves projecting messages from the brain to the body's mechanisms. In other words you consciously 'think' of one part of your body releasing away from another part. There are two kinds of directions, and these are often referred to as 'primary directions' and 'secondary directions'.

PRIMARY DIRECTIONS

Alexander found that stress-related problems can be traced to over-tensed neck muscles that interfere with the freedom of the head in relationship to the neck and spine. If this relationship is interfered with it will be impossible to obtain any lasting freedom elsewhere in the body. The primary directions, given below, allow the reflexes and muscles throughout the body to work as they should.

· Think of your neck being free so that your head goes forward and up, in order for your back to lengthen and widen.

It is important that these directions are given in this sequence, as it is impossible to allow your head to go forward and up if you have not released the tension in your neck. Likewise, it is impossible to achieve the beneficial lengthening of the spine if your head is not going forward and up.

· Allow there to be freedom of your neck.

The pivot point of the head is located at the top of spine and is much higher than many people realise. The centre of gravity of the head is situated forward of the pivot point, which means that the head is naturally inclined to move in a forward direction. The purpose of this direction is to release the excessive tension that often exists in this area, which causes the head to be pulled back and down on to the spine, thus interfering with the natural balance of the head. It is important to realise that neck tension may be difficult to detect, because often we have become used to the feeling over a long period.

· Allow your head to go forward and up.
You should think of your head going in a direction that is forward and up in relation to your spine, and not to your environment. Most of our five senses are situated in the head, and because of this the body mechanisms are arranged in such a way that the head leads a movement and then the body follows. Allowing the head to go forward helps this natural organisation to occur, allowing all our movements to be performed with the greatest efficiency.

· Allow your back to lengthen and widen.
This direction will help you to reduce tension throughout the upper part of your body. Expanding this area will improve your breathing and allow the internal organs more space, enabling them to function more efficiently. It will also help to prevent a shortening of the spine, which can cause or aggravate back and neck pain. Releasing tension in the upper part of your body will also ease the downward pressure which causes unnecessary restriction in the hips, legs and feet, and makes standing and walking more difficult. By thinking of your back lengthening and widening, your spine will be encouraged to elongate rather than to shorten, and this is often accompanied by a feeling of lightness and ease.

SECONDARY DIRECTIONS
As a supplement to the primary directions, secondary directions can help to release tension in localised parts of your body. Some common secondary directions which can be useful in reducing levels of stress are shown below:

· Allow your shoulders to release away from one another.
This will help anyone with rounded shoulders or who has shallow breathing or asthma.

· Allow your left shoulder to release away from your right hip, and your right shoulder to release away from your left hip.
Leaning over a school or office desk for many years can often cause a slumped posture. This direction can be very helpful in releasing the tension caused.

· Think of allowing your hands to widen as your fingers lengthen. This can help anyone who unconsciously clenches their fists when under stress.

· Think of allowing your to jaw drop away from your ears. This will help to release tension in the jaw muscle, which is common to those under stress.

· Think of your feet spreading on to the ground as your toes lengthen. This can release tension in the toes and will help you to stand and walk with more poise.

These are just a few examples of the many directions that Alexander devised. For all the directions it is important to think of one part of your body moving away from another part, as this allows a lengthening of your entire being. This works against muscle tension, which by its very nature causes the muscles concerned to shorten.

While you can try these out at home while lying down (see Chapter Two) initially most people *do* the directions rather than just *think* of them – this will only increase muscle tension and defeat the purpose of the exercise. It is highly recommended that you have some Alexander technique lessons in order for a trained teacher to help you understand these directions correctly.

Visiting an Alexander technique teacher

The length of time a lesson will last varies from teacher to teacher, but the average is between 30 and 45 minutes. The number of lessons that will be needed can vary from person to person, depending on how stressed you are. A basic course will consist of between ten and thirty lessons. In cases of severe stress, it may be advantageous to have two lessons a week for the first two or three weeks, but later on when you are more familiar with the principles of the technique you may only need a lesson once every two to three weeks.

What takes place during an Alexander technique lesson will vary depending on your own requirements and the way your teacher chooses to put across the information. If a friend has not personally recommended the teacher, it is worth having one lesson from two or three different teachers to see which one suits you best. Various organisations will supply a list of qualified teachers and their details can be found in the useful addresses section at the end of this book.

Since teachers have different styles, the following account of an Alexander technique lesson is only a guide to what to expect.

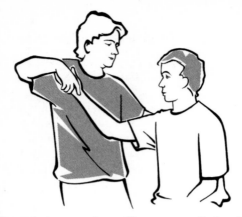

The Alexander technique teacher will move your limbs slowly to find excessive tension.

Your first lesson

This lesson may be slightly longer than subsequent lessons. You may be asked if you have any medical problems and the state of your health in general, your teacher may also want to know why you have come for lessons and what your expectations are. A teacher will often take a few minutes to discuss the principles and history behind the technique. After this he, or she, may gently move your limbs or head and ask you not to help while she checks your body for excessive muscle tension.

When tension is found, your teacher will make you aware of it and will then tell you what 'direction' you need to think of in order to let the tension go. This may be done while you are sitting, standing or lying on a treatment table. At the end of your first session your teacher will advise you as to how many lessons you are likely to need and over what period of time.

During your first lesson you may experience a feeling of lightness, or experience your body moving with greater ease. This sensation may only last for a short time to begin with, but with subsequent lessons it will last for longer and longer periods.

When you have learnt how to let go of the existing muscle tension that has accumulated in your body over a number of years, you will begin to learn new ways of moving which will help to prevent the tension from returning. You will relearn ways of walking, standing, sitting and bending which put less strain on your body and result in a reduction of stress.

Benefits of the Alexander technique

The Alexander technique helps you to be aware of and let go of excessive muscular tension, which in turn can help to eliminate stress-related disorders such as backache, headaches, insomnia, as well as a whole range of other physical aches and pains. By learning to use this Technique you will achieve a greater ease of movement, feel calmer and gain a greater control over your own life.

The experience of the Alexander technique can never be described in a book or conveyed by speech. It is a wonderful feeling of lightness and ease that allows all parts of the body to work in unison with each other. It gives many people a sense of peace and oneness that they had forgotten was possible. Some people describe the feeling as 'walking on air'. It is simply the feeling of letting your body work as nature intended without the interference that is practically universal in Western society today. Many people also find that their confidence and self esteem grow, and with it a new-found spontaneity, a greater contentment and a deeper love of life. These qualities are the natural antidote to stress. A self-help procedure of the technique can be found in Chapter Two.

Aromatherapy

'Smell the perfume of flowers, taste with relish each morsel.
As if tomorrow you could never smell and taste again.
Make the most of every sense.'
HELEN KELLER

What is aromatherapy?

Aromatherapy is a natural treatment which uses concentrated pure oil extracts from plants, herbs, grasses and fruits. These essential oils have the ability to relax, balance, rejuvenate, restore or enhance body, mind and spirit. Skilful blending by an aromatherapist balances the therapeutic effect and aromatic quality of individual essential oils.

Aromatherapy is thought to aid the self-healing processes by working indirectly on the body's systems. The results of aromatherapy are very individual. While there is general agreement about the actions of certain oils, aromatherapists may describe the properties and characteristics of an essential oil in varying ways. This is perhaps because no two people are affected by the same essential oil in exactly the same way. It is even possible for the same person to be affected differently by the same oil at different times, according to the surroundings, the time of day or the person's mood.

History of aromatherapy

The history of healing with essential oils has often been confused with the origins of herbalism or perfumery. Herbalism deals with the healing powers of the whole plant and perfumery is the non-medical use of aromatic substances.

It is thought that the use of Aromatherapy predates written history. Essential oils and fragrant plants were used in some form – for pleasurable, medicinal or ceremonial reasons – in many ancient civilisations. There is documented evidence of how the Ancient Egyptians used aromatic plants and their oils to create massage oils, medicines, embalming preparations, skin care products, fragrant perfumes and cosmetics. There is also evidence of aromatic oils being used many thousands of years ago in Africa, India and China. Other ancient cultures of North and South America such as the Indian, Aztec, Inca and Mayan people used aromatic plants and oils in ceremony and in daily life. However, it is not exactly clear whether in ancient times these people were performing the art that could just as easily fall into the categories of herbalism or perfumery.

Aromatherapy, as we know it today, was started in the early part of the twentieth century by a French chemist, Rene-Maurice Gattefosse who coined the term 'Aromatherapy' in 1928. One of the discoveries he made was after burning his arm in his laboratory. He plunged his arm into vat of lavender water as it was the only cold liquid available to him at the time and he was amazed to find that not only did he get tremendous relief, but the wound healed quickly and with little scarring. In this way he was inspired to investigate the healing properties of other essential oils.

During the 1950s Aromatherapy became established in Britain through the work of an Australian woman, Margurerite Maury. Working in the beauty industry, she became interested in the ability of essential oils to penetrate the skin and preserve youth. Her cosmetic use of essential oils was used in her beauty salons where beauticians started to give massages using aromatic oils for skin care and relaxation.

In 1964, another French medical doctor Jean Valnet, inspired by Gattefosse's research, published his own work, *The Practice of Aromatherapy* and then in 1977, Robert Tisserand released his book *The Art of Aromatherapy*. Both of these works were successful in capturing the great interest in the subject that we see today.

How does aromatherapy work?

When inhaled, essential oils can affect the body in several ways. As the essential oil vapours enter the nasal passages, they stimulate the olfactory nerve which sends messages directly to the part of the brain concerned with memory, learning and emotion. The inhalation of the essential oils can trigger changes, which can stimulate physiological responses within the body via the nervous, endocrine or immune systems. Either stimulation or sedation of body systems or organs may occur, influencing emotional and hormonal responses.

It is thought that because of the sedating or stimulating effect that the essential oils have on the brain and the subsequent effect on the nervous system, essential oils can also indirectly raise and lower blood pressure and possibly aid in balancing hormonal secretion. The inhalation method can also be useful for respiratory symptoms. Aromatherapy aids relaxation which invokes a feeling of calmness so that an emotional balance is restored.

Using aromatherapy oils

The application of these essential oils may be in the form of inhalation, compresses, bath additives, vaporisation or with the combined benefits of massage.

INHALATION

This is an excellent way of using the oils if you have a cold, sinus problems or general congestion caused by stress. Add two to four drops of essential oil to a bowl of steaming water, cover the head with a towel, close the eyes and breathe in the vapour for several minutes. Please note that asthmatics and allergy sufferers should use this method only under medical advice.

COMPRESSES

This can be a very effective way of easing muscle spasm, for example headaches or period pain. A compress may either be used hot or cold depending on what you are treating. If you are using a combination of the two, you should start with a hot compress and finish with a cold. Use two to eight drops of essential oil depending on the size of the area to be covered.

Fill a container with warm water, add the chosen oils and mix well. Fold a towel to approximately the size of the area to be treated. Lower the folded towel on to the water until the bottom layer is wet. Place the towel moist-side down over the affected part of the body and leave in position for at least 15 minutes.

Try lavender or peppermint for headaches and lavender or marjoram for period pains (a condition that is exacerbated by stress).

BATH ADDITIVES

This is a wonderful way to relax and unwind after a busy day and enjoy the therapeutic properties of essential oils. Add between three and nine drops of your chosen essential oil to a bath of hot water. Stir the surface and soak for at least 15 minutes. This allows the oil to penetrate the skin while the vapour is being inhaled. Do not use shampoo or soap at the same time as this may neutralise the beneficial effects of the oil.

Try rose or marjoram for muscle stiffness. Lavender can help greatly with general relaxation and is excellent for those who suffer from insomnia due to stress.

VAPORISATION

This is the easiest way to enjoy oils. You can create your own mood, remove unpleasant smells or even enhance concentration while working. Add up to six drops of essential oil to a saucer of water and place on a radiator. Alternatively, use a special burner with a night light as the source of heat, or you can buy special rings to place on a light bulb. Within a few minutes the room will be filled with the aroma of your choice.

MASSAGE

This is the most effective method of reducing stress, by combining the relaxing properties of certain oils with the therapeutic power of touch. The oils should be diluted with an odourless carrier oil such as grapeseed, sweet almond or peach kernel.

Always use natural oils. Synthetic oils, even if chemically similar, will lack all the natural elements that make essential oils so valuable therapeutically. You may also get a nasty reaction to the synthetic components in the chemicals.

The addition of synthetic chemicals is not normally disclosed in the essential oil business, so unless there is a declaration that the oils are natural, pure and unadulterated, assume otherwise.

Buying and storing essential oils

Where possible buy quality oils from a qualified aromatherapist who can advise you about the full potential of the oil. Essential oils are affected by sunlight, and should only be sold and stored in dark glass bottles with sealed caps. Always make sure that the cap is on securely and the bottle stored upright in a cool dark place, as the oils are highly volatile and will evaporate easily. Never store essential oils in plastic bottles as they can evaporate through certain types of plastic or can even start to react with the plastic. Never buy essential oils with plastic droppers in them for the same reason. It is important to note that some oils, such as rosemary or peppermint, may not be suitable during pregnancy. All oils should be stored out of children's reach.

Essential oils should be stored in a cool place away from sunlight.

Aromatherapy oils for stress

This just a small selection of essential oils available – they are the most commonly used oils for stress and stress-related ailments.

BERGAMOT – This is an uplifting oil for those under excessive tension at work or any other kind of stress. It can also work as an antidepressant. Do not use if you are going to be exposed to strong sunlight or a sun-bed as it can sometimes cause permanent skin pigmentation.

CHAMOMILE – A calming oil, chamomile is suitable for any nervous conditions or insomnia.

FRANKINCENSE – A good oil for many kinds of stress or nervous conditions as it can help to relax and revitalise. It can be very useful for those who face new situations or who want to let go of the past. Not suitable for babies or small children.

GERANIUM – This is another calming oil that helps to balance the emotions. It is a good tonic for those who are feeling low and is one of the best oils to use when suffering from the effects of stress. Not suitable for babies or small children.

GRAPEFRUIT – This can act as a natural antidepressant as it can quickly clear unwanted thoughts. Not suitable for babies or small children.

JASMINE – This is a luxurious oil which can be helpful to those who suffer from nervous tension, depression, menstrual problems, laryngitis, anxiety or lethargy. The sheer luxury of its rich scent uplifts the spirit. This is one of the more expensive oils. Not suitable for babies or small children.

JUNIPER – This oil is very useful for those who suffer from fatigue. It can help to lift negative energy. Not suitable during pregnancy, for babies or small children.

LAVENDER – This is another oil that acts as an antidepressant – it will help you to relax and is good for insomnia. Can be especially good for those who overwork or suffer with muscle fatigue.

LEMON – This refreshingly uplifting oil can be very useful for tension headaches. It may in some cases cause skin irritation. Not suitable for babies or small children.

MANDARIN – This oil acts as a natural tranquilliser and can help those people who suffer with insomnia, nervousness, liver problems or anxiety. Not suitable during pregnancy, for babies or small children.

MARJORAM – This is another helpful oil to aid relaxation and can help to reduce high blood pressure. It can also help those who have menstrual problems, anxiety, asthma, insomnia and circulation or muscular disorders. A good one for the bath. Not suitable during pregnancy, for babies or small children.

ORANGE – Another uplifting oil for those who suffer from depression, lack of energy, anxiety or nervous conditions. Not suitable for babies or small children.

PEPPERMINT – A cool and refreshing oil which can to help relieve headaches or migraine. Not suitable during pregnancy, for babies or small children.

ROSE – Another luxury oil for relaxation which can help depression, headaches and insomnia. It is nurturing and comforting which is the perfect choice for an overworked person. Not suitable for babies or small children.

ROSEMARY – A stimulating oil for those with muscular conditions, depression, fatigue, memory loss or migraine. It can help to refresh and enliven the spirit and can aid concentration. Not suitable during pregnancy, for babies or small children.

SANDALWOOD – A natural sedative which aids relaxation.

TANGERINE – An uplifting oil which can help those in shock.

VALERIAN – This is a very calming essential oil that helps the following nervous conditions: trembling, neuralgia, insomnia and palpitations. It is a natural sedative or tranquilliser.

VETIVER – Another calming oil which is helpful for those who suffer with anxiety, nervous tension or insomnia.

YLANG YLANG – This is a helpful oil for those with high blood pressure due to anxiety.

Stress reducing oils at a glance

The following oils are in order of which works best, however if you don't like the smell of certain oil just pick one further along the list.

- Anger – Chamomile, Ylang Ylang, Geranium, Frankincense

- Anxiety – Bergamot, Lavender, Orange, Ylang Ylang

- Depression – Sandalwood, Bergamot, Rose, Lavender

- Fatigue and Nervous Exhaustion – Peppermint, Rosemary, Sandalwood

- Headache – Chamomile, Lavender, Peppermint

- High Blood Pressure – Lavender, Marjoram, Ylang Ylang

- Insomnia – Chamomile, Lavender, Marjoram

- Loss of Appetite – Bergamot, Orange

- Migraine – Lavender, Chamomile, Peppermint

- Nervous Tension – Bergamot, Chamomile, Lavender, Sandalwood

- Pre-menstrual Tension – Jasmine

- Shock – Lavender, Orange, Peppermint

- Stress (general) – Bergamot, Chamomile, Frankincense, Lavender, Sandalwood, Vetivert

This chart is intended to be a simple guide. For more detailed information or treatment you will need to contact a qualified aromatherapist. The addresses of national organisations can be found at the back of this book.

Chiropractic

'The cure of disease lies within the body.'
HIPPOCRATES

What is chiropractic?

The word chiropractic comes from the two Greek words, *cheir* meaning 'hands' and *prakikos* meaning 'done by'. A chiropractor diagnoses, treats and helps to prevent mechanical disorders of the joints. Chiropractic is based on the premise that there is an integral relationship between the muscular, skeletal and nervous systems. Chiropractic maintains that a dysfunction of the musculo-skeletal system will cause an abnormality in the nervous system which, of course, can lead to problems in other systems of the body.

The definition of Chiropractic is 'a science that is concerned with the relationship between structure (primarily the spine) and function of the human body (primarily co-ordinated by the nervous system).' If this relationship is not in harmony then it can affect the restoration or preservation of health. Chiropractic tries to correct the misaligned bones or muscles in order to remove any interference to the body's own healing abilities. Chiropractors direct their attention mainly to the spine, searching for an area which is deviant from normal. Any deviation or malpositioning of a spinal vertebra may cause a neurological imbalance within the body.

For the past 100 years, people of all ages have benefited greatly from chiropractic's drugless, non-surgical approach to better health. By removing interference on the nerves around the spinal column, and sometimes from other joints as well, chiropractors can help patients achieve and maintain good health, and improve physical performance.

History of chiropractic

Chiropractic is a modern health practice with historical roots. Ancient Egyptian and Chinese works of art illustrate spinal manipulations, and in the fifth century BC, the great philosopher Hippocrates developed theories of spinal mechanics and the role of manipulation in the overall health of the human body.

Dr Daniel David Palmer, the founder of the chiropractic movement, was a self-educated magnetic healer, who had a large practice in the booming river-boat town of Davenport, Iowa, USA. Dr Palmer made his first discovery in 1895, when he delivered the first ever chiropractic adjustment to his janitor, Harvey Lillard. Harvey had been deaf since a childhood accident in which he hurt his back. During the accident Harvey claimed that his neck had audibly 'popped'. After only that one adjustment from Dr Palmer, Lillard made a full recovery including the total restoration of his hearing.

After this incident with Lillard, Palmer immediately recognised the relationship of spinal displacement and the poor functioning of the nervous system and began his study of the workings of the spine. Eventually, using the bony processes used for muscular attachments and movement, he learnt to lever the spinal vertebrae back into position and free the full nerve flow to the body. After successfully manipulating many of his patients he began teaching these ideas to others. Since then chiropractic has dramatically grown as a healthcare profession, with over 50,000 doctors now practising in the US alone.

Visiting a chiropractor

Chiropractors are physicians who give particular attention to the relationship of the structural and neurological aspects of the body. A chiropractor is trained in physical examination, orthopaedic and neurological testing, radiographic interpretation and direct palpation of joint movement, and can therefore determine any areas of the spine that are not functioning properly. He or she has an intimate knowledge of human neurology and bio-mechanics and an understanding of the many different problems resulting from neuro-musculo-skeletal dysfunction.

A chiropractor applies a controlled and directed pressure, known as a chiropractic adjustment, to restore the spine's ability to function. The purpose of the adjustment is to correct spinal problems that may interfere with the flow of nerve impulses to and from the brain as any interruption of this communication pathway can produce pain and illness. Depending on how chronic the problem is, the chiropractor may apply one or a series of adjustments to re-establish proper joint movement. By correcting musculo-skeletal problems of the spine in its early stages, a chiropractor can assist in the prevention of more obvious and advanced disorders and can help the patient to heal while tissue damage is still minimal and reversible.

Like osteopathy, chiropractic is a hands-on therapy and through massage manipulation techniques, a chiropractor can treat people with stress-related problems.

Your first consultation may last for about 30 to 60 minutes, depending on the chiropractor. It will start with an interview between you and your therapist during which you will be asked about your physical and emotional health, and details of any medicines you are taking. Most chiropractors will want to assess your posture, so they often ask you to undress down to your underwear so as to make the most accurate diagnosis possible. He or she may then ask you to stand, walk up and down, lean forward, backward and to each side in order to study your posture and movements.

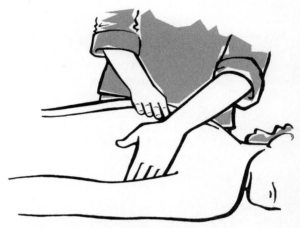

A chiropractic high-velocity adjustment can bring instant relief from pain.

During the examination the chiropractor will focus on your reflexes, muscle strength and flexibility. He or she will often do additional investigations such as an x-ray. The treatment will start there and then.

During the treatment you will be asked to lie on a special table and the chiropractor will start to massage the muscles that have become tight. The treatment will then include soft-tissue stretching and joint movements. Your treatment may end with a high-speed manipulation of a bone or bones in the spine. This swift movement can be very effective in freeing a joint that is causing trouble. This often reduces pain and improves mobility very quickly, but you may feel an ache or be tender for some time afterwards.

It should be noted that joint manipulation techniques are sometimes not suitable for children and elderly people.

Benefits of chiropractic

Chiropractic can be effective in treating stress-related problems such as headaches, breathing disorders, irritability and back pain.

Headaches

Recurring headaches are one of the most common modern afflictions. The two main types of headache that chiropractic can treat are tension headaches and migraine.

Tension headaches are more common and are often caused by worry or stress. Chiropractic can relieve the pressures that cause your muscles to tighten. Migraine headaches can be caused or exacerbated by stress. Migraines produce strong throbbing pain and sometimes nausea. A disturbance of energy flow between the brain and spinal nerves to the various functions of the body may produce a headache when triggered. Chiropractic treatment can restore a natural flow.

Breathing disorders

Often breathing disorders, such as asthma and allergies, can be caused by physical interference along the nervous system. Chiropractic manipulation will often relieve these types of symptoms.

Irritability

Mental stress is a more common cause of physical discomfort than most people realise. People suffer from many kinds of mental stress caused by nervousness, anger or just life in general. Mental stress may lead to physical stress and poor health. When we experience nervousness, fear, anger or anxiety, muscle tension is also increased.

Back pain

Back pain can often be a symptom of stress. Chiropractic can be useful in relieving the problem, but without changing your stress levels the problem will only return. Alexander technique lessons in combination with chiropractic treatment can be very effective.

Chiropractic can help relax the muscles and realign the bones, relieving the physical stress, and relaxing nerve pressure. Other stress-related conditions that may be helped by this therapy are digestive problems, fatigue and insomnia.

For this treatment it is essential that you consult a qualified practitioner – addresses may be found at the back of this book. There are no self-help techniques available for this therapy.

Hypnotherapy

What is hypnotherapy?

The word hypnosis comes from 'Hypnos', the Greek god of sleep. A hypnotic trance is not sleep, though it sometimes seems to resemble it, it is a state of deep concentration which causes an altered awareness. This is usually achieved with the aid of another person, although it can also be self-induced. The hypnotic trance state is a perfectly natural phenomenon, we all undergo trances from time to time – when we are pre-occupied with what we are doing or when we are completely absorbed in music, a memory, day-dreaming or watching a play or a film. During these times we can lose touch with our surroundings and not notice the passing of time. These are everyday examples of natural trance states. It is the utilisation of this altered state of awareness that is used to suggest ideas of self-improvement or desired changes of behaviour.

Hypnotherapy is gaining acceptance by the general public as physicians and dentists are beginning to use it in their practice. As the hypnotic trance is a naturally occurring state it is possible for most people to be hypnotised if they so choose. Hypnosis produces a state of increased awareness and alertness while feeling relaxed and focused. You can hear everything that is said while in a trance and are in control at all times.

Hypnosis is defined as a temporary state of awareness in which the conscious mind is relaxed and a person has access to the potentials of their unconscious mind. This trance state allows your subconscious mind to accept suggestions that can help to increase your self-confidence and allow your creative abilities to emerge. Hypnotherapy can also help you to remove any features of your character which you feel are undesirable.

Although there have been cases in which hypnotherapy has had amazing results, it is not really a miraculous power. Hypnotherapy is merely a technique which enables your mind to use your own natural abilities to produce healing results. According to a study carried out by the World Health Organisation, nine out of ten people can successfully be hypnotised. Those who are motivated and are willing to make a change in their lives are usually the most successful subjects. People with a strong desire to be in control, particularly those who have disorders such as anorexia or obsessive compulsive disorder, are hard to hypnotise.

History of hypnotherapy

The history of hypnotherapy dates back thousands of years and spans the globe. Chinese medicine used medical procedures that were of hypnotic nature. At a later date the ancient Greeks used techniques similar to hypnosis to cure anxiety and hysteria. The Druids used what they called the 'magic sleep' to cure warts. Through the ages magic, voodoo, shamanism and faith-healing have often included hypnosis in some form or another.

One of the most influential individuals to practise hypnosis was a Viennese physician by the name of Frank Anton Mesmer. In the late eighteenth century Mesmer successfully treated a large number of people by putting them into deep trances. He induced a trance through a series of passes made over the body with his hands or magnets, and referred to his technique as 'mesmerism'. Working with a person's psychic and electromagnetic energies, he performed mesmerism on many people across the world. Although he was very successful, his fondness for theatrical settings soon alienated the medical community. The medical journal *The Lancet* referred to Mesmer as a 'quack' and 'impostor', but even today we still use the phrase 'to mesmerise'.

Another founder of modern hypnotherapy was a French doctor named Ambroise Liebeault. He realised that once in an hypnotic trance, his patients were receptive to the suggestion that they were recovering from their ailments and that he could therefore help them to heal themselves.

James Braid, a Manchester surgeon who coined the term hypnotism, brought hypnotism to the UK in the late nineteenth century. Although, initially, he was strongly opposed to mesmerism, he gradually became interested in the subject and began studying it. He claimed that cures were not due to psychic and electromagnetic energies, but merely to suggestion and he developed the eye fixation technique of inducing relaxation which became known as hypnosis. He also realised that ideas could be implanted while in the hypnotic state. However the medical establishment were still unimpressed.

One of the best known people to use hypnosis was Sigmund Freud. He employed it to enhance the effects of the suggestions he would make to eliminate his patients' psychiatric symptoms. Later he became more and more convinced that psychiatric symptoms often represented the unconscious memories, feelings and inner conflicts of the patient so he began to use hypnosis to investigate the subconscious mind. Although these methods often seemed to produce satisfactory improvements in the condition of the patients, the effects were often short-lived.

Hypnosis was not actually approved by the British Medical Association committee until 1955 and by the American Medical Association until 1958. Doctors now use it as an alternative to anaesthetics and hypnosis has now become a well established part of current medical, dental and psychological practice. It is considered to be a valuable therapeutic aid.

Today in the UK psychologists and doctors practise hypnosis in the NHS, but it is used more widely in the United States, Australia, Sweden and Japan.

How does hypnotherapy work?

No one knows really knows how hypnotherapy works. One explanation is that it calms and reassures the patient and that this has a general beneficial effect. Another theory is that under hypnosis the left analytical side of the brain switches off allowing the right, non-analytical, side of the brain to take over. It is well known that psychological factors play an important part in causing diseases of all sorts, ranging from cold sores to cancer. Doctors now realise that our health and emotions are closely related. Through the process of hypnosis, the mind focuses positively on issues, mental or physical, and eliminates any unwanted thoughts. Whether the problem is a disease, stress, fear, or any other kind of issue, hypnosis can help to overcome it.

If a person is stressed, the brain sends negative messages to the immune system which affects the organs throughout the body. On the other hand, if a person is in a humorous or optimistic mood, this stimulates the immune system, increasing its ability to attack cancer cells, infectious diseases, allergies and other immune illnesses. The hypnotherapist aims to replace the negative thoughts of their client with positive ones thus directly affecting the mental, physical and emotional well-being of the person.

The brain

The brain is the body's most extraordinary organ – it is the seat of the intellect and the interpreter of our senses. It controls every single thing we do, the thoughts we have, the movements we make and everything we feel. The brain controls all the incredible functions of the body that keep us alive. It stores all the memories we have ever had and these can be retrieved under certain conditions.

The brain has two hemispheres, the right and the left. The left hemisphere is the conscious or the reasoning mind and the right hemisphere is the subconscious mind which accepts what is impressed upon it without any judgement.

The left hemisphere of the brain is used for the following:

- Consciousness
- Reason
- Language
- Writing
- Ego

- Logic
- Mathematics
- Reading
- Analysis

The right hemisphere controls:

- Unconsciousness
- Rhythm
- Creativity
- Dreaming

- Recognition
- Visualisation
- Synthesis
- Emotions

(For people who are left-handed, the opposite is the case.)

When the unconscious and conscious minds are in conflict, the unconscious mind usually wins. For example, in the case of smoking, people's conscious intellect knows this behaviour is destructive but their unconscious feelings often win, and they continue to smoke even though they know that it is bad for them. When the intellect takes over to express feelings, our unconscious mind can often become intensely negative, leading to feelings of depression. Hypnotherapy aims to bring our feeling and subconscious mind into alignment with our intellectual and conscious mind.

Visiting a hypnotherapist

During your first session the hypnotherapist will take a full medical history, explain what hypnosis is and how it can be useful to you. The first session usually lasts 60 to 90 minutes and the average number of sessions needed to produce a result will probably vary between six and twelve. These will usually take place weekly, depending on the condition being treated.

During hypnosis the therapist will encourage you to disengage yourself from your surroundings and help you to focus on imagery, thoughts and feelings. When you are in a relaxed state the therapist will make suggestions, perhaps accompanied by an image, or ask you to imagine things. If, for instance, you are suffering from stress you might be asked to imagine yourself sunbathing on a tropical island or swimming in a cool, crystal-clear ocean. Hypnotherapists sometimes plant a post-hypnotic suggestion that your stress will lessen as the week goes on.

When you are hypnotised, you are in a peaceful state of relaxation. While in this state, your mind is open to suggestions. You are, however, fully aware of what is going on around you and you respond only to suggestions that are beneficial to you. Relaxation is the first and most important phase of hypnosis. Your eyes should be closed and your breathing should be steady and deep.

When in a relaxed state, tension is released from your muscles, which allows the nervous, respiratory and circulatory systems to calm down. This state of relaxation is the key to overcoming fears or habits that you may have. If a negative thought enters your mind just let it go. While you are in a deep state of peace your mind is clear of other thoughts that might have been troublesome or irritating.

A new belief system can be created with suggestion which replaces an old outworn one which is no longer serving you. This is done by putting a positive image in your head to replace existing negative thoughts. The hypnotherapist can freely implant whatever ideas he, or she, wishes into your subconscious mind. Suggestion is the fundamental basis of hypnosis, and it plays a significant role in nearly every aspect of treatment.

Benefits of hypnotherapy

Hypnotherapy can be beneficial for a variety of physical and psychological disorders and stress-related conditions. Memory and learning ability can be improved through the use of hypnotherapy and individuals can learn to relax and build self-confidence. Children can be treated for bed-wetting and asthma. Hypnotherapy can also be used to treat addictions such as smoking and over-eating and social problems such as stammering and blushing, phobias, panic attacks and obsessions.

Hypnotherapy can be used to make people less aware of pain in various conditions – from tooth extractions to giving birth. Under hypnotic suggestion wounds are stitched, fractures set and burns dressed.

However, it is important to realise that, occasionally, hypnotherapy can be harmful to people with certain psychiatric disorders such as schizophrenia, severe depression and personality disorders. Hypnosis may bring about an emergence of strong and disturbing feeling from the patient's past. For that reason, it is always best to place yourself in the hands of a qualified and reputable hypnotherapist.

Osteopathy

'Medicine should begin with the patient, continue with the patient and end with the patient.'
ANDREW TAYLOR STILL

What is osteopathy?

According to the General Osteopathic Council:

'Osteopathy is an established, recognised system of diagnosis and treatment, which lays its main emphasis on the structural and functional integrity of the body. It is distinctive by the fact that it recognises that much of the pain and disability which we suffer stems from abnormalities in the function of the body structure as well as damage caused to it by disease.'

The word 'osteopathy' is a combination of the Greek word *osteo* meaning bone and *pathy* meaning suffering.

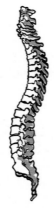

Osteopathy is concerned with the structural and functional integrity of the body.

104

An osteopathic treatment is concerned with the relationship between the structure of the body – the skeleton, muscles, ligaments and connective tissue – and the way in which the body moves and functions. It is a natural system of diagnosis and treatment. To an osteopath, the body functions as a complete, working system, so any problems affecting its structure upset the balance of general health. For this reason, an osteopath will not simply want to ease the pain and stiffness in your neck, but also want to know what is causing that pain, which could be stress or mental anxiety.

Contrary to the meaning of the word, osteopathy is not just about bones, as easing muscular tension also plays a considerable part. Osteopaths work on the principle that if a muscle is in tension it becomes less elastic, and therefore more prone to damage. Over-tense muscles slow down the circulation and lymphatic systems, so that the body's growth and elimination processes are restricted. They inhibit heart function and can worsen the effects of common respiratory conditions, such as asthma.

History of osteopathy

Andrew Taylor Still, the originator of osteopathy, was born in Lee County, Virginia, in 1828. He trained as a doctor, but followed a different path from many of his peers, refraining from the habit of administering drugs in huge quantities. He became further disillusioned with medicine when three of his children died of viral meningitis, and this encouraged him to seek out new methods of treating sickness. Still saw that tension in muscles and misaligned bones places unnecessary strain on the body, and that this strain can be caused by emotions like anger and fear caused by stress. He firmly believed that adjusting the framework of the body could ease physical strain, so that the systems within it would run smoothly and the body could heal itself. Still considered the vertebrae of the spine to be particularly important as they protect the spinal cord – a major part of the nervous system. He knew that the nervous system penetrates every area of the body, controlling voluntary and involuntary movement and registering every sensation. Still believed that anything interfering with the nervous system could resonate throughout the body and by treating the spine other areas of the body would be affected.

When Still was 45 years old he announced osteopathy to the world. In 1892 he organised a school in Kirksville, Missouri, to teach osteopathy to others, and it was from these small beginnings that osteopathy became widely known.

Visiting an osteopath

Like chiropractic, osteopathy is a hands-on therapy. Through touch, massage, manipulation and stretching techniques, an osteopath can diagnose and treat people with physical and emotional problems.

The details of your first visit depend almost entirely on the type of osteopath you choose. But with any practitioner, your first consultation will last for about 45 to 60 minutes. It will start with an interview between you and your therapist, during which you will be asked details about your physical and emotional health, your home, work and lifestyle and the names of any medicines or remedies you are taking. Most osteopaths will want to assess your posture, so they may ask you to undress to your underwear so as to make the most accurate assessment possible. You may then be asked to stand, walk up and down, lean forward, backward and to each side, or sit as you would normally sit at your desk or at home, while the osteopath studies your posture, movements and how you usually hold yourself.

The osteopath may also put you through a series of specialised mobility exercises and will check the alignment of your spine. These extensive testing procedures will focus on your reflexes, muscle strength and flexibility. The osteopath may need to carry out additional investigations such as x-ray or blood tests to give you a full diagnosis and suitable treatment plan. If the osteopath believes that he or she can help you the treatment may begin there and then. If not you may be referred to a colleague, to another therapy, or back to your doctor.

During the treatment you will be asked to lie on the therapist's table and he or she will often start with a deep massage to relax the muscles. The treatment will then include soft-tissue stretching and joint movements. Often your treatment may end with a high velocity adjustment or 'thrust'. This is a swift movement that can be effective in freeing a joint that is not moving correctly or in reducing pain and improving mobility. After a treatment that involves joint manipulation you may ache or feel tender for a few hours.

As with chiropractic, joint manipulation techniques are not suitable for everyone. Children and elderly people are generally treated with more gentle release techniques such as massage or cranial treatment.

What is cranial osteopathy?

Cranial osteopathy, or cranial-sacral therapy as it is sometimes known, is a gentle and powerful component of osteopathic medicine, which uses the patient's own inherent forces to overcome strains within the body. Cranial treatment is a subspecialty of conventional osteopathy, performed by an osteopath and often may be more appropriate for the relief of stress.

Removing any restrictions in the flow of the cranial fluids helps to balance the body's energy.

By using very gentle manipulation cranial osteopathy helps to restore the free flow of cranial fluid throughout the cranial sacral mechanism. A cranial osteopath places a very light touch on your head, spine and sacrum, examining the cranial rhythmic impulse to find the areas of the body where the impulse is restricted. The physician works by applying very gentle manual techniques and gently unwinds any strains present within the system. When this happens, the patient may feel a slight sensation where the physician's hands are placed, otherwise there is no sensation of pain while they are performing these gentle manipulations on your head or sacrum. An osteopath may work for half an hour or longer and by doing so will help to remove any restrictions and restore normal flow of the cranial fluid. During cranial treatment the patient may feel so relaxed that they drop off to sleep.

Benefits of osteopathy

Like chiropractic, osteopathy can help to relieve many stress-related aches and pains such as back pain, breathing disorders, headaches and irritability.

Back pain

Back pain can be often caused by stress. An osteopath can help to realign bones to give you temporary relief, however any good osteopath will also advise you about changing your lifestyle.

Breathing disorders

Stress is a major factor in the cause of breathing disorders. Osteopathy can help sufferers to breathe more easily and is therefore particularly beneficial to those who have asthma.

Headaches

Recurring headaches are one of the most common symptoms of stress. The two main types of headache that osteopathy can treat are tension headaches and migraines. Tension headaches are often caused by worry or stress and by relieving the tension in your muscles osteopathy can help you to become more relaxed.

Migraines are headaches that produce severe pain, nausea and disturbed vision. Like tension headaches, migraines can also be caused or exacerbated by stress. Through conventional and cranial osteopathic treatment a reduction of tension in the head, neck and spine can be achieved.

Irritability

Mental stress caused by dealing with life's problems can often lead to physical stress and poor health. Osteopathy can relax muscles and realign the bones, thus relieving physical stress and relaxing nerve pressure throughout the body.

Other stress-related conditions which may be helped by this therapy are digestive problems, fatigue and insomnia.

For all of these treatments it is essential that you consult a qualified practitioner – addresses may be found at the back of the book. There are no self-help techniques available for this therapy.

Reflexology

'Take rest;
A field that has rested gives a beautiful crop.'
OVID

What is reflexology?

Reflexology is a special type of foot and hand massage, based on the principle that there are reflex zones in the feet and hands which correspond to different areas of the body. These zones are connected to specific organs and systems via a network of nerve pathways which exist throughout the body. It is believed that by applying pressure to these zones you can bring the body back into balance and good health. Reflexologists apply specific pressures using thumb, finger and hand techniques which are performed without oils, lotions or creams. The physical act of applying precise pressure helps to release blockages that inhibit energy flow and cause pain and disease. This pressure is believed to affect internal organs and glands by stimulating numerous reflex points that exist in the feet and hands.

Reflexology works on the basis that the body has the ability to heal itself. Due to illness, stress, injury or disease, the body gets into a state of imbalance, and vital energy pathways become obstructed, preventing the body from functioning effectively. When any of these pathways become blocked, the body may experience different levels of discomfort or 'dis-ease'. Reflexology may assist in reviving one's energy flow and bringing the body back into a state of balance. It can help to maintain the body's natural equilibrium, thus aiding the body's own healing processes. Reflexology can also be an aid to diagnosing more serious problems.

History of reflexology

Reflexology is not new – it is thought to have existed for many thousands of years and has its origins in ancient Egypt, China and India. The earliest evidence exists in the form of Egyptian hieroglyphs on the walls of a pyramid dating from between 2500 and 3000 BC. These drawings which show people having their hands and feet massaged are thought to be the first known documentation of the therapy we know today as reflexology. There is also further evidence in ancient texts of China and India where references were made to reflex areas of the feet.

The scientific basis to reflexology began in the last century when during the 1890s research scientist and medical doctor, Sir Henry Head demonstrated the neurological relationship that exists between the skin and the internal organs. The Nobel prize-winner, Sir Charles Sherrington later proved that the whole nervous system and body adjusts to a stimulus when it is applied to any part of the body. About the same time in Germany, Dr Alfons Cornelius observed that pressure to certain spots triggered muscle contractions, changes in blood pressure, variation in warmth and moisture in the body as well as directly affecting the mental state of the patient.

In 1913 Dr William Fitzgerald, an American ear, nose and throat surgeon, introduced reflexology to the West. He recognised that pressure on specific parts of the body could have an anaesthetising effect on a related area. Developing this theory, he divided the body into ten equal and vertical zones, ending in the fingers and toes. He deduced that pressure on one part of a zone could affect everything else within that zone.

In the early 1930s, a physiotherapist named Eunice Ingham studied the response of different areas of the body to zone therapy. The feet, which proved to have the greatest level of sensitivity, were most responsive. Ingham performed intensive study on the physiology and responses. Tender spots were discovered when the feet were probed by precise thumb pressure upon certain areas. Ingham then began equating these spots with the anatomy of the human body, thus devising a map of the feet that exactly mirrored the body. For example when the big toes are treated there is a corresponding effect in the head. In this way a complete massage of the whole foot can have a relaxing and healing effect on the entire body. Her method was then named the 'Ingham Method of Massage Compression,' which later became known as the 'Original Ingham Method of Reflexology.'

Today, reflexology is practiced by nearly twenty-five thousand practitioners around the world and is a safe and simple way to induce relaxation and a genuine sense of well-being.

How does reflexology work?

No one really knows for sure how reflexology works although reflexologists have developed several theories for why this therapy is so effective. One theory states that when messages are sent along nerve pathways from the brain or spinal cord to any area of the body, a minute amount of waste is produced. This waste often contains lactic acid, uric acid, calcium and various other organic and inorganic by-products. When a muscle or organ is over-stressed, as is the case during illness or at times of extreme pressure, these waste products build up and block energy and circulation. Since the feet are the lowest point in the body gravity itself may be responsible for carrying this waste along the nerves to the lowest extremities: the hands and feet. During the course of a session the therapist aims to break up these deposits by applying therapeutic pressure.

Another theory states that a reflexology treatment helps to increase circulation, allowing additional blood and oxygen to flow around the body which helps to relax muscles and flush toxins from organs. And yet another hypothesis is that energy is transferred from the therapist to the client and that the client's stress is drawn out by the therapist's healing abilities. This may account for the exhaustion that is sometimes felt by the therapist after a particular session when a client has been under a tremendous amount of stress.

Another explanation is known as the meridian theory which states that the meridian points are affected through the practice of reflexology (see the sections on shiatsu and acupuncture in this chapter). The end result is the removal of obstructions to the body's natural flow of energy and an achievement of balance and improved health. Regardless of how the treatment works, having your feet massaged is very calming for most people and therefore has a direct effect on stress levels.

Visiting a reflexologist

On your first visit there is a preliminary talk with the practitioner. The reflexologist then begins to work on your feet or hands, noting any problem areas. In the West only pressure from the therapist's hands is used, whilst in Asia implements are also used and the finger pressure is much firmer. There may be discomfort in some places, which is an indication of congestion or imbalance in a corresponding part of the body. Any discomfort is short-lived and for the most part the treatment is pleasant and soothing. Different people may have different reactions to a treatment and the application of the therapy is unique to each practitioner.

Usually a reflexology session lasts for about one hour. A course of treatment varies in length depending on your needs and your reflexologist will discuss this with you at the first session. Both patient and reflexologist must be positioned comfortably to ensure maximum relaxation. Usually, the patient prefers a reclining position. A reflexologist normally works on the bare feet, but occasionally when this is not possible for some reason, the treatment can be given on the hands. The practitioner will hold your right foot firmly but sensitively, and will begin kneading it, loosening each toe and relaxing the foot's many muscles, tendons, bones and ligaments. This stimulates thousands of nerve endings. The reflexologist's thumb systematically probes the inner sole of the foot, crossing the ball of the foot, up to the toes, covering every part of your foot and ankle. Your left foot is then relaxed in the same way. All of the reflex points on both feet are always stimulated.

After the first treatment or two your body may respond in a very definite way. Many people have a feeling of well-being and relaxation, but occasionally some people may feel lethargic, nauseous or tearful, but these feelings are only transitory. It is, however, vital information for reflexologists, as it shows how your body is responding to treatment. In general people are amazed by the simplicity of reflexology and baffled by the results produced by merely applying pressure to the reflexes in the feet and hands.

Self help

Unlike many other therapies you can help yourself by using simple reflexology techniques. Many people are unable to reach their feet in comfort, but exactly the same reflex points are mirrored in the hands. Take either hand, and using your other thumb, apply pressure to the reflexes in your hands. Using firm pressure, massage each area in a circular movement bending the thumb at the first joint. Be sure to work the reflex areas on both hands. When working a tender area you may come across crystal-like deposits under the skin.

Better still, let a friend or spouse give you a gentle foot massage. Sit back in your favourite recliner and remove your shoes and socks. Have your partner release the tension in your feet by using a motion similar to lightly wringing out a towel around the entire foot. The chances are that they will stimulate many of the zones.

Although reflexology may not be the complete answer for someone who is suffering from chronic stress, it can be a useful tool in the fight against stress.

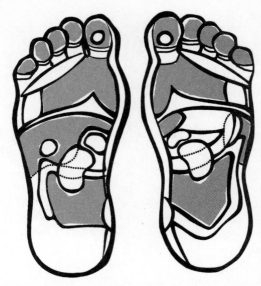

The feet's reflex zones correspond to the body's organs and systems.

The individual reflex areas on the feet correspond to different areas of the body:

- metatarsal (balls of the feet) – chest, lung and shoulder area

- toes – head and neck

- upper arch – diaphragm, upper abdominal organs

- lower arch – pelvic and lower abdominal organs

- heel – pelvic and sciatic nerve

- outer foot – arm, shoulder, hip, leg, knee and lower back

- inner foot – spine

- ankle – reproductive organs and pelvic region.

Shiatsu

*'Great energy only comes from a correspondingly
great tension between opposites.'*
CARL JUNG

What is shiatsu?

Shiatsu is a Japanese healing art deeply rooted in the philosophy and practices of Traditional Chinese Medicine, incorporating the therapeutic massage of Japan. The word 'shiatsu' comes from two Japanese words: *shi* meaning finger, and *atsu* meaning pressure. The technique involves the application of gentle pressure using the thumbs, palms and elbows, along the energy channels in the body which are known as meridians. Shiatsu has evolved from ancient Chinese healing practices which promote the body's own healing abilities.

Shiatsu is growing in popularity and stature as quickly as any complementary health therapy today. It can be used whether you are ill and want to get better, or if you are well and wish to stay that way. Shiatsu not only does the patient a lot of good; it is also pleasant to give.

History of shiatsu

In the tenth century Japanese monks began to study Buddhism in China. They observed the healing methods of Traditional Chinese Medicine and took them back to Japan. The Japanese not only adopted these methods, but also began to enhance them by practising new combinations, eventually achieving a unique Japanese treatment called shiatsu. Shiatsu combined the principles of Traditional Chinese Medicine with techniques that are similar to acupuncture, but without using needles.

The origins of shiatsu stretch back into an untold history of its use in the Japanese home. Well into this century it was still a treatment that a rural mother would use to treat regular day-to-day ills in her family, probably in combination with local herbs and other folk wisdom. She would also teach what she knew to her daughters, and so knowledge would be passed down from generation to generation.

In the early 1970s, a few Japanese practitioners came to the United States and Europe to teach shiatsu to Westerners, and since then it has become an increasingly popular practice in the West.

How does shiatsu work?

As outlined in the sections on acupuncture and Chinese medicine, our bodies have energy circulating through them and this energy is more concentrated in certain channels called meridians. These meridians do not directly correspond to any anatomical component recognised by Western medicine. The energy that flows along the meridians is known as Ki in Japanese. Just as electricity flows through electrical wires, this energy flows through us, nourishing our muscles, blood vessels, nerves, bones, vital organs and glands.

The best way to understand the flow of Ki through the meridians is to compare it to the flow of blood in our veins and arteries. If our blood does not reach our toes, they become cold. If our blood does not flow freely, we have high or low blood pressure. If our blood clots, we have an embolism or a stroke. Similarly, unbalanced or stagnant Ki can cause many diseases and ailments. In fact, Traditional Chinese Medicine is based on the principle that every illness, ailment and discomfort in the body can be explained in terms of an imbalance of Ki.

Each meridian is related to one of the five elements. For example, the heart meridian is related to the element fire, the kidney and bladder to water. Along the meridians are pressure points or 'gateways', special places where Ki can become blocked. With the help of a trained practitioner, its flow can be freed and balance restored. It is when this energy becomes stagnated that we experience problems with our health. Shiatsu promotes the flow of energy and eliminates the blockage of the Ki. The causes of Ki blockages or stagnation are varied but the more common ones in society today include stress, overworking, limited exercise, poor posture, trauma and lack of sleep or rest. Our polluted environment and low quality of food, along with bad habits and negative emotions, such as fear, depression and anger, can also interfere with the flow of Ki.

Visiting a shiatsu practitioner

Shiatsu is typically carried out with the client on a futon (a firm Japanese mattress which is placed on the floor). Both the practitioner and the client wear loose comfortable clothing and the treatment is done in a series of positions – sitting and lying on the back, front or side. The practitioner uses his, or her, own body weight rather than muscular effort, to create pressure, so shiatsu is less tiring for the practitioner than other forms of bodywork. The most frequently used techniques are broad overall preparatory stretches, followed by more particular work leaning with the palms, plus the most specific method, thumb work on local pressure points. On occasion, pressure from elbows, knees or other parts may also be used. In these ways, the practitioner is able to correct the body's internal energy.

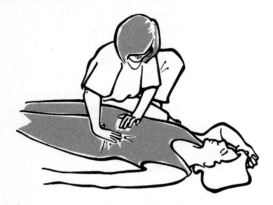

The practitioner uses their body weight rather than muscular pressure to trigger pressure points.

Gentle pressure is applied to the meridians found mostly on the back, legs, arms, neck, head and abdomen, although the focus of the treatment will vary depending on the individual's needs. Shiatsu is not meant to be painful although some areas can be a little tender. It is not unusual for the client to drift into a state of relaxation and fall asleep. No needles, creams, machines or other devices are needed for the experience of a complete shiatsu session. The practitioner uses gentleness, fluidity and rhythmical motion to work with the imbalances in the client's Ki.

The shiatsu practitioner consciously tries to be aware of the client's breath and to be respectful of their essential being. The practitioner's hands become sensitive as they feel the Ki energy in the body; they may feel places where there is excessive energy or places where the body is lacking energy. They apply pressure and patiently wait for the moment of release and then the natural healing flow is restored. In the practice of shiatsu, each person is primarily responsible for his or her own health and well-being. This contrasts with the Western belief that the medical practitioner is principally responsible for our health.

Benefits of shiatsu

Chronic stress can be relieved by stimulating the flow of energy along certain meridians, which induces deep relaxation. The energy which flows up and down these channels takes many and various forms. It is important to be open to an understanding of Ki which can at times manifest itself as muscle tone, while at others as blood flow, lymphatic fluid, hormones or enzymes.

Receivers of a shiatsu treatment, irrespective of their belief in the concept of Ki, can expect to feel very different at the end of a treatment. This may just be a profound form of relaxation or could be an entirely different state of being. Certainly the effects of a treatment may continue for some time afterwards, with changes often only taking place in subtle ways.

Shiatsu therapy is generally most effective as a course of treatment over a number of weeks and most shiatsu therapists are likely give the receiver advice on helpful lifestyle changes, particularly in respect to diet and exercise. As well as addressing particular problems, shiatsu treatment will usually also help you to restore energy, release tension, promote relaxation and generally enhance a feeling of well-being.

8

complementary medicine

'Everything that you need exists in this present moment,
and this moment is all that exists.'
KEN CAREY

As with the alternative therapies covered in the previous chapter, complementary medicine is becoming increasingly popular with patients who have either found no effective cure within conventional medicine or who are just looking for a new way of healing. These methods are often seen as safer, less costly and more natural ways of treating the body. The medical establishment is also starting to accept complementary remedies and some doctors either recommend these medicines themselves or will refer a patient on to someone else who is trained in their use. Four areas of complementary medicine are covered in this chapter:

- Bach flower remedies

- Chinese herbal medicine

- Herbal medicine

- Homeopathy

Bach flower remedies

'Health depends on being in harmony with our souls.'
DR EDWARD BACH

What are Bach flower remedies?

The Bach system consists of 38 prepared tinctures. Each is made from a healing plant or flower. There are two methods used to make the Bach flower remedies. The first is for the more delicate flowers, which are prepared using what is known as the sun method. This involves floating the blooms in pure water for three hours. The second method is used for woody plants, or flowers which bloom when the sun is weak, and these are prepared by boiling in water for half an hour. In both cases full-strength 40 per cent brandy is used as a preservative, mixed in equal quantities with the prepared tincture. Drops from the preserved mother tincture are further diluted in brandy to make the stock bottles that can be bought in the shops.

History of Bach flower remedies

Dr Edward Bach (1886–1936), the originator of the Bach flower system, began his career as a medical doctor and bacteriologist. He studied medicine at University College Hospital, London and worked in Harley Street as a doctor. Later in his career he worked on vaccines as a pathologist, and it was during this time he became increasingly interested in homeopathy.

Despite the success of his work with orthodox medicine he felt dissatisfied with the way doctors were expected to concentrate on diseases without really considering the mental or emotional state of the patients. He was inspired by his work with homeopathy but wanted to find remedies that would be purer and less reliant on the products of disease. Although he lived in London he spent much of his time in the country. He noticed that when he became stressed, a walk in the countryside would help him to calm down. During these walks he also noticed that he would be attracted to certain flowers and shrubs which helped restore in him a feeling of well-being. So in 1930 he gave up his lucrative Harley Street practice, determined to devote the rest of his life to a new system of medicine that he was sure could be found in nature.

At this time Dr Bach abandoned the scientific methods he had used up until then and chose to rely on his natural gifts as a healer and on his own intuition to guide him. He firmly believed that a healthy mind is the key to recovery from ill health. During his observations and research he became convinced that the dew on the flowers was impregnated with their medicinal properties. He subsequently gave these remedies to his patients and noted their reactions.

Slowly he discovered the remedies he needed to complete his system, each aimed at a particular mental or emotional state. He began to spend much of the spring and summer looking for and preparing the remedies, and during the winter he gave help and advice to those in need of it. He discovered that when he treated the personalities and feelings of his patients their unhappiness and physical distress would be alleviated as well. The body's natural healing abilities would be enhanced and the patient's symptoms would start to abate. He could foresee that he would be unable to fulfil the demand for his remedies by merely collecting the dew, so he started to experiment by floating freshly picked flowers on clear spring water in sunlight.

In 1934 Dr Bach moved to Mount Vernon in Oxfordshire. It was in the lanes and fields nearby that he found further flowers, which completed the set of remedies that are used today. During this time he experimented on himself and would often suffer the emotional state that he needed to cure and then try various plants and flowers until he found the one single plant that could help him. He did this by using his imagination to invoke the emotion he wished to find a cure for and in this way, through great personal suffering and sacrifice, he gradually developed the Bach flower system.

Dr Bach passed away peacefully on the evening of 27 November 1936. He was only 50 years old, but he had left behind him a system of medicine that is now used all over the world.

Using Bach flower remedies

Bach flower remedies are simple to use and Dr Bach designed his system so that anyone could use them without medical training. The tinctures can be bought from most health food stores or natural medicine shops. Bach flower remedies are safe to use for babies, children or animals. Most are used regularly over a period of weeks or months, although some remedies can be used now and again to deal with temporary problems or set-backs. There are no adverse side effects and an overdose is impossible.

Dr Bach believed that each person was a certain 'type' and that there was an ideal remedy to suit each of these types. In order to try Bach flower remedies to combat stress, first read through the list of appropriate personality types on pages 122–124. Think about your emotional and mental state, your habitual reactions and your attitude towards other people and life in general, and then select one of the remedies. If you cannot decide on one, you can use up to seven remedies at the same time, but if at all possible it is better to use them one at a time.

Once you have decided on the right remedy, you need to make up a treatment bottle. Take a 30ml dropper bottle (available from most chemists) filled with spring water and add four drops of each tincture you wish to use. Four times a day, drop four drops from the treatment bottle into a glass of water to drink, or alternatively place the drops straight on to the tongue. Store the treatment bottle in the fridge. If a 30ml dropper bottle is difficult to obtain, a slightly smaller or larger one will do just as well.

For short-term problems you should feel the effects within a few minutes, or at least within half an hour. For long-term problems, improvement may take two or three weeks. It is important to note that other people may notice the change before the person who is taking the remedy.

Be patient and continue with the treatment for at least three weeks. However, if there is no effect you have probably chosen the wrong remedy. Do not worry – no harm has been done – just go back to the list of remedies and try again.

How do Bach flower remedies work?

It is very hard to explain scientifically how Bach flower remedies work, but many thousands of people have experienced the benefits of these remedies. Anyone who has stood in a garden and smelled the roses, jasmine or honeysuckle knows how soothing and invigorating the experience can be. There is nothing tangible about the feelings, yet the effects are undeniable. Bach flower remedies work in exactly this way.

According to Bach, certain flowers are of what he called a 'higher order' and as a result have a greater power than ordinary medicinal plants. The 28 healing plants that make up his system deal with the disharmony within the mental and spiritual aspects of our being and have the power to transform negative emotions such as fear, anger or hatred into strength, love and joy. In this way they work by addressing the root cause of the illness. In a similar way to homeopathy Bach flower remedies can be thought of as gentle catalysts that generate change from within. Dr Bach described his healing system in the following way:

'The remedies cure, not by attacking the disease, but by flooding our bodies with the beautiful vibrations of our Higher Nature, in the presence of which, disease melts away as snow in the sunshine.'

Bach flower remedies for stress

AGRIMONY – For those who hide mental torture behind a cheerful face. This remedy can be useful for those who are restless at night or who resort to drink or drugs while under stress.

ASPEN – For people who are stressed due to fears that are of an unknown origin.

BEECH – For those who are intolerant. This remedy is helpful for those who are annoyed by the actions, habits or gestures of others, or perfectionists who are obsessed with order or discipline.

CENTAURY – For those who become stressed because they are timid, weak-willed or subservient to others. It can help those who feel that they are a doormat and unable to say 'no'.

CERATO – This remedy is for the worrier. It is particularly helpful to those who seek advice and confirmation from others as they lack trust in their own decisions.

CHERRY PLUM – This remedy is given to those who fear their mind giving way. It can be helpful for those who are desperate or who are on the verge of a nervous breakdown. It is also given to those who fear suicide, losing control or insanity.

CLEMATIS – For those who dream of the future and have a lack of interest in the present. These people can be heavy sleepers or fall asleep easily. This remedy can be useful for those who avoid life's difficulties by withdrawing.

ELM – Very helpful for those who are overwhelmed by responsibility or for those who suddenly doubt their own abilities.

GENTIAN – For those who feel discouraged after a set-back or for those who feel depressed because of a known cause. It can be useful for children who are discouraged at school.

GORSE – Very helpful for those who have overwhelming feelings of hopelessness and despair. These people believe that nothing more can be done and therefore feel it is useless to try to find a solution to their problem.

HORNBEAM – For people who feel tired at the thought of doing something – they often have that 'Monday morning feeling'. They suffer from mental fatigue and doubt their own ability to cope, but they usually accomplish the task at hand.

IMPATIENS – This remedy is useful for those who feel impatient, irritable or nervous. They suffer mental tension through frustration, as everything has to be done quickly. Other people doing things slowly irritates them.

LARCH – For those who suffer from a lack of confidence; they feel inferior and are convinced of failure and feel that they cannot do as well as others. Can be useful to take before exams or tests of any kind.

MIMULUS – For those people who have a fear of known things; they are often timid or shy and blush easily. These people may suffer with a stutter or stammer.

MUSTARD – This remedy can be useful for those who experience descending gloom for no apparent reason. They have feelings of hopelessness, despair or depression that come suddenly and then lift just as quickly.

OAK – This remedy is for the plodder who keeps going past the point of exhaustion – they overwork and hide their tiredness, but can end up having a nervous breakdown.

OLIVE – For people who feel completely exhausted following mental or physical effort. These people have suffered long under adverse conditions or have little vitality as a result of a long illness. This remedy is great for those who give themselves no time for relaxation or to enjoy life.

PINE – For those who feel guilt, and blame themselves for the mistakes of others. They overwork as they are over-conscientious, but they are rarely content with their achievements.

RED CHESTNUT – This type of person is over-concerned for the welfare of loved ones. They over-worry and always fear the worst.

ROCK ROSE – For those who are stressed from an accident or near escape – they have feeling of panic, terror and fright. Can be very useful for those who suffer from panic attacks or nightmares.

ROCK WATER – For individuals who are rigid, self-repressed and have very strong opinions, or who deny themselves life's pleasures. Often they are perfectionists.

STAR OF BETHLEHEM – For those who are in shock or suffering from the delayed reaction that shock can bring. This remedy is extremely helpful for those who are stressed after they have had sudden bad news or a grievous disappointment.

SWEET CHESTNUT – For people who are experiencing extreme mental anguish and have reached the limit of their endurance, and feel that they have almost been destroyed. This remedy is useful after bereavement or divorce or when a person feels that everything has been tried and there is no hope left.

VERVAIN – This is a good remedy for stress as it is for those who are often tense and unable to relax. It is helpful for those whose mind is always running ahead and who are inclined to tackle too many jobs at once. Other symptoms include sleeplessness due to hyper-anxiety, being highly strung or over-enthusiastic. They have a strong sense of justice and commitment.

WALNUT – This remedy is for those who need protection from change and unwanted influences. These folk are often over-sensitive to atmospheres and the ideas of others.

WHITE CHESTNUT – This remedy is for those who are preoccupied and lack concentration or for those who are tormented with unwanted thoughts and mental arguments. It can help to prevent persistent thoughts from going around and around.

WILD OAT – This remedy is for those who are uncertain about their direction in life and as a result can feel despondent or dissatisfied.

WILD ROSE – For those people who are apathetic or feel that they are drifting through life. They feel weary and lacking in vitality, yet they are resigned to their illness or problems and fail to realise that they have actually created these conditions in the first place.

There is also a very helpful combination remedy called Rescue Remedy which is a composition of Cherry Plum, Clematis, Impatiens, Rock Rose and Star of Bethlehem. This remedy is given for any kind of shock, sudden bad news, panic attacks, marital or family problems, taking exams or if you are under any kind of stress at work.

Chinese herbal medicine

'Knowing ignorance is strength.
Ignoring knowledge is sickness.'
LAO-TZU

What is Chinese herbal medicine?

Like acupuncture, the use of Chinese herbs is another important part of Chinese medicine. Chinese medicines are derived from animal, plant and mineral products although in most cases herbal formulas are used. Remedies such as cinnabar, amber, bears' gall, mahuang and ginseng are very common in China yet most people in Western society are unfamiliar with them. When visiting a herbalist for minor complaints such as headaches or colds Chinese people would go into a pharmacy and buy herbal medicines over the counter – these come in tablet or liquid form. For more serious complaints people would visit a doctor of Chinese medicine who would fill out a prescription in much the same way as Western doctors. Then the pharmacist will choose a few particular ingredients from the thousands that they have in stock. The patient then takes the ingredients home, boils them into a 'soup', and consumes the mixture.

History of Chinese herbal medicine

Chinese herbal medicine is thought to be more than two thousand years old and much of this ancient medical knowledge has been preserved in books. Many of these works have now been translated into several languages, and have exercised a profound influence on East Asian and European countries. One of the best known of these Chinese medical works, the *Matura Medic*, was compiled in the Ming Dynasty (AD 1368–1644). It includes descriptions of 1,892 different kinds of medicines and is still used to this day.

All of the remedies have been tried and tested over the centuries. According to one Chinese legend, Shen Nung, the leader of an ancient clan, took it upon himself to test, one by one, hundreds of different plants to discover their nutritional and medicinal properties. Over thousands of years other Chinese have used themselves as guinea pigs in this same way to continue testing plants for their properties of inducing cold, heat, warmth and coolness. They classified the medicinal effects of the plants on the various parts of the body, then tested them to determine their toxicity and what dosages would be lethal. This accumulation of experience strengthened the Chinese understanding of natural principles in Chinese medicine.

How does Chinese herbal medicine work?

As mentioned in the section on Acupuncture in Chapter Seven, the Chinese have a very different system of classifying illnesses. The first principle is that of 'yin and yang' which can be thought of as two opposing forces – yin being the passive or receding aspect of nature and yang in contrast being the active or advancing aspect. Yin and yang are opposing forces yet they also depend on each other for their existence and thus cannot be thought of independently. Stress causes an imbalance in the yin and yang energies and the aim of Chinese medicine is to restore this balance.

This imbalance occurs because a person has either too much yang or too little yin. In some cases there could be just the right amount of yang but a person could have used up a lot of their yin due to many late nights, working too hard, worry, too much sex or a variety of emotional problems. If there is not enough yin, it doesn't necessarily mean there is too much yang, it's just that the yang qualities – being outgoing, talkative and restless are more obvious. This imbalance can be restored by building up the yin with rest, good nutritious food, meditation, T'ai Chi or Qi Gong.

When the yin is at normal levels and yang energies are greater than they should be then you can get such stress indicators as migraine, manic behaviour, high blood pressure, sweating, red face, bloodshot eyes or constipation. In order to reduce stress levels the balance between yin and yang has to be restored. See also the section on acupuncture (page 76).

These are some practical ways of moving towards a yin way of being:

- Slow down all of your actions
- Go for a swim
- Read a good book
- Have a massage
- Lie in the dark while listening to beautiful music
- Rest

· Go for a leisurely stroll

· Eat slowly

Visiting a Chinese herbalist

For minor ailments you can buy herbal remedies at most health food or Chinese food shops and, like Western medicines, correct dosage will be stated clearly on the packet. For an in-depth treatment you will need to visit a qualified Chinese herbalist and information on how to find one can be found on page 151.

The attainment of equilibrium in the body's flow of energy (Qi) and the re-balancing of yin and yang are the guiding principles of Chinese medicine. These principles give the herbalist a better understanding of the patient's illness and may suggest improvements in the patient's life.

As with acupuncture, the prescribing of Chinese herbal medicine is based upon an individual diagnosis using the techniques of pulse and tongue evaluation in conjunction with the reading of other symptoms or personality traits to form a unique pattern diagnosis. This is because the flow of Qi and balance of yin and yang can be affected by a person's living environment, their life rhythms, the foods they prefer or avoid, their personal relationships, their language and the gestures they use.

Chinese herbal medicine is concerned with treating the underlying condition and rarely causes unpleasant or harmful side effects. Once the excesses or imbalances of the body's function have been pinpointed, they can be adjusted by using different herbs to restore the balance of the person's physical and mental health.

All the Chinese herbal remedies on sale in the West have been analysed and tested, for their effectiveness and then carefully prepared in the appropriate concentrated dosages. Chinese medicine is now used as a form of treatment for a multitude of ailments ranging from colds and flu to chronic fatigue. Chinese herbal remedies are also known to be very effective in the relief of mental and emotional conditions such as anxiety, depression, stress and insomnia.

Chinese herbal remedies for stress

This information is designed as a quick guide if you are mildly stressed and is not intended to replace the advice of a qualified Chinese herbalist.

Ginseng

This is probably the most famous Chinese herb and can be bought in most health food shops. In oriental medicine ginseng is considered a superior medicine because it restores vital energy while balancing organ functions. It has been used in China for thousands of years, and ginseng remains a main ingredient in hundreds of herbal formulas prescribed today.

The three types of ginseng most commonly cultivated and marketed today are Chinese or American ginseng, Korean ginseng and Russian or Siberian ginseng. It is important to note that these three ginsengs come from completely different plants.

CHINESE OR AMERICAN GINSENG – American ginseng is considered to be the most balanced. It serves as both a yin and a yang tonic. It counteracts weakness, irritability and fatigue associated with low grade fevers.

KOREAN GINSENG – This has been used in oriental medicine for over 4000 years as a Qi tonic. It is ideal for weak, chronically ill patients suffering from exhaustion and anxiety. However it is best reserved for people over 40 years old and should not be taken by people suffering from high blood pressure. It should not be taken for more than a few weeks at a time as over-use can cause imbalances.

RUSSIAN OR SIBERIAN GINSENG – This amazing herb helps the human body adapt to stress and normalises all its functions. It is used by athletes to enhance endurance and performance. It enables them to recover faster after strenuous exercise. This herb can be ingested over a long period of time – up to eight months.

This ginseng is preferable if you are under stress; it also helps to protect from environmental pollutants and enhances the immune system. A good quality Siberian ginseng tincture can be taken over a period of months by any age person to increase physical energy and endurance and help the body cope with stress. This should probably be bought from a practitioner or a good health food shop which carries Chinese herbs.

DANG SHEN (CODONOPSIS) – This is a sweet, soothing herb which is less expensive than ginseng. It strengthens the immune system, lowers blood pressure and fights fatigue. Dang shen is considered a good herb to treat normal day-to-day kinds of stress and fatigue.

MU LI (OYSTER SHELL) – This is a substance long used in oriental medicine to calm the spirit. It is good for restlessness, irritability, insomnia, palpitations accompanied by anxiety, headaches, blurred vision or night sweats.

SUAN ZAO REN (ZIZYPHUS SEEDS) – These come from the Chinese date. They are good for insomnia, irritability and palpitations accompanied by anxiety. If people experience anxiety or stress, they can munch on a teaspoon of these seeds two or three times per day.

GE GEN (KUDZU ROOT) – Oriental medicine has used this herb to treat alcohol abuse, as it has proved effective in suppressing cravings for alcohol. It also relaxes muscle spasms particularly in the neck and shoulders and lowers blood pressure. You can use it as a thickener for sauces instead of cornflour.

Herbal medicine

'There is much to find of nature's way.
It is with you always, available to you always.
Take the time to hear and see that which is close at hand.
There are forces in you untried.
They are yours to be used as you find them.'
JOHN AND LYN ST CLAIR-THOMAS

What is herbal medicine?

Herbal medicine is probably the oldest form of therapy in the world and every different culture has its own form of herbalism. Both humans and animals throughout history have been drawn to plants to cure their ailments. Herbal medicine can be used to treat a great variety of illnesses and even up until this century it was the mainstream medicine. Certain herbs seem to have healing powers which can have a dramatic effect on the body when prescribed in the right way. However it is important to note that other herbs can have unpleasant or even dangerous side effects if the recommended dose is exceeded or if they are used inappropriately.

The action of the individual herb is not imposed upon the body systems in an aggressive or suppressive fashion as is sometimes the case with modern drugs. They are chosen to bring the body into a state of harmony and balance which is then maintained. The herb supplies the body tissues with the nutrients to build, repair and restore their normal function. Many of the causes of imbalance in the body are caused by a build-up of toxins due to the under-function of the organs of elimination such as the liver or kidneys. Therefore, using herbs to stimulate the cleansing action of the colon, lymph, lungs and skin can help the detoxification of the body.

History of herbal medicine

The use of healing herbs goes back beyond written history. It is probable that primitive man would have seen the benefits of herbs by watching the instinctive behaviour of animals. Over time these early people would have deduced that certain plants were beneficial for specific ailments.

One of the first records of the use of herbal medicine dates back to the Greek and Roman civilisations. They wrote down detailed information about the use of herbs and Hippocrates, the famous Greek doctor listed over 400 herbs which were used in healing. The great philosopher Aristotle also studied the use of herbs and their effect on the body in the fourth century BC.

When the Romans invaded Britain they brought many of their own native herbs with them and these herbs and the knowledge of their use were integrated into the herbal lore that already existed. During the reign of Henry VIII (1509–1547), herbal medicine was formally established throughout England by an Act of Parliament and even today, England is the only country in Europe in which herbalists can practise freely. The next major influence in herbal medicine was brought about because the explorations during the reign of Queen Elizabeth I (1558–1603), when many herbs from the American continent were introduced into England.

One of the best known herbalists was Nicholas Culpeper who published *Culpeper's Herbal Remedies* in 1653. He associated certain herbs and plants with certain planets although most of this knowledge has now been lost. Because of this astrological link herbalism was often criticised by the Church over the centuries and this was partly why herbalism fell out of favour as newer, more scientific medicine became into being.

During the 1970s, interest in herbalism was rekindled and this new growth was encouraged by the World Health Organisation, although herbal remedies are still rejected by some people as rooted in the superstitions of the past. Even to this day the selling of herbs in many American states is illegal. Generally though, herbal medicine is on the increase and the number of herbalists in the Western world is growing fast. In 1994 the Medicines Control Agency in the UK told herbal medicine suppliers that by 1 January 1995 every herbal remedy would have to be licensed, which would have meant the closure of many suppliers' businesses. This move was eventually dropped because of the unexpectedly high number of people writing to the government objecting to the plans and it is very likely that herbal medicine will gain even more popularity in the twenty-first century.

Visiting a herbalist

If you have consultation with a herbalist, a case history will be taken which includes your family history, details of any past illnesses and your present complaint. Your first session will probably last anything up to one and a half hours during which time you may be asked about the nature of your work, leisure time activities, eating habits, your emotional state and whether you are taking any medication. All this information will help the herbalist understand any physical, circumstantial and environmental factors contributing to your particular health problem. The herbalist will also need to get to know you as a person, where the underlying emotional tensions are, how you react to stress, your experiences and what external circumstances affect you. This again helps them to form a complete picture of you as a patient and allows for a truly holistic treatment. As herbalists are trained in conventional medical diagnosis, there is also likely to be physical examination, much the same as a doctor might perform. He or she will check your pulse and breathing rate, take your blood pressure and perform any necessary examinations.

At the end of the session the herbalist will prescribe a herb or a selection of herbs for your specific condition. There are thousands of herbs that a herbalist can choose from although most will use about 200 of the more common ones. Herbalists will often prescribe tinctures (herbs in alcohol and water), or syrups (made by boiling the herb in water and adding sugar as a preservative). Occasionally they may administer the herbs in the form of teas, poultices or ointments. They may give you advice on diet and lifestyle too.

Subsequent visits to the herbalist will last between 45 minutes and an hour and you will usually be seen at three-weekly intervals. It can take about two to three months to get a significant improvement in your condition. You are unlikely to feel ill after taking a herbal medicine, but some people do get an unexpected reaction. If this is your experience, phone the herbalist immediately and he or she will probably be able to identify which herb is causing you problems and may change the prescription.

How does herbal medicine work?

Herbal remedies are free of additives and preservatives and are perceived by many people to be far safer than orthodox medicine. A large number of orthodox medicine's most potent drugs, however, are actually based on plant remedies – the most well-known of these being aspirin and penicillin. Aspirin consists of an ingredient that is similar to the bark of a willow tree and penicillin was derived from the deadly nightshade plant.

There is a wide variety of herbs each having a definite medicinal purpose, but they may be divided into the following categories:

- alteratives – help to cleanse the bloodstream

- anti-spasmodics – prevent the recurrence of muscular spasms

- astringents – help to condense tissues which have become too lax

- demulcents – help to soothe or cool inflamed or injured tissue

- relaxants – help to relax the body

- stimulants – stimulate a system that has become sluggish

- tonics – generally strengthen the whole system.

Creating a herbal formula for a patient requires a knowledge of the causes of the underlying problem and since we are all affected by emotional states, a truly holistic treatment must take these into account. Herbalism is not a self-help therapy and therefore it is always vital that you consult a qualified herbalist before taking any of the remedies. However, once you are familiar with the herbs many of them can be safely and frequently used on a daily basis for relaxation. A number of remedies come in the form of teas and can be purchased at most health food shops.

Many people mistakenly assume that all herbal products are safe because they are 'natural', however, the Department of Health (UK) has identified some plants that carry a potential risk. These include pennyroyal and broom, which can cause miscarriage; bearberry and ragwort, which have been linked to liver damage; and feverfew, which may cause mouth ulcers. In 1993, comfrey tablets and capsules were withdrawn from sale in the UK because they may cause liver damage.

Another common error that people make is that because herbal medicines are good for you, you can take as much as you like. However, this is simply not the case and like conventional medicines an excessive intake could be toxic. Having said that, herbal remedies are relatively safe as long as you follow the following guidelines:

- Do not exceed the stated dose. Some herbs can have grave side effects if taken in large doses

- Do not pick herbs yourself unless you are sure that you know what to look for

- Only buy a herbal remedy if the package states clearly which herbs it contains

- Never buy herbs or herbal products abroad

- Telling a poisonous plant from a non-poisonous one is not easy

- Do not buy herbal over-the-counter remedies for serious illnesses. Always consult your herbalist or doctor.

- Never buy herbal products by mail order.

- Stop using a herbal remedy immediately if you start experiencing side effects

- Do not take herbal remedies for prolonged periods.

If you are pregnant or are breast-feeding, in general do not use herbal remedies. If you do want to do so, ask your doctor or a qualified medical herbalist first.

Herbal remedies for stress

The variety of herbs is vast, and a qualified herbalist should always be consulted, but the following remedies may help in the treatment of stress-related conditions.

- CHAMOMILE – is useful as a calming remedy
- DANDELION – acts as a cleanser for the body

- ECHINACEA – is used to help strengthen the immune system

- ELDERFLOWER – helps to combat mild flu

- FEVERFEW – can be used to treat migraine

- GARLIC – is beneficial for a range of diseases including high blood pressure and arthritis

- GINKGO BILBAO – helps the action of neuro-transmitters in the brain and improves blood flow. It is also thought to be beneficial in cases of tinnitus

- GINGER – can help nausea and may give relief for colds and flu

- HAWTHORN – is beneficial in the treatment of congestive heart failure

- LIME FLOWER – is effective as a relaxant

- MISTLETOE – is used to treat cancer

- PEPPERMINT – is good for headaches

- ST JOHN'S WORT (HYPERICUM) – has been shown to be effective in the treatment of depression

- VALERIAN – may be used for insomnia.

Homeopathy

'Homeopathy cures a greater percentage of cases than any other method of treatment. Homeopathy is the latest and most refined method of treating patients economically and non-violently.'
MAHATMA GANDHI

What is homeopathy?

Homeopathy is a scientific system of health care which can help to activate the body's own healing processes in order to cure disease naturally, gently and safely. Homeopaths believe that the human body is closely interconnected mentally, emotionally and physically, and must be treated as such. Homeopathy uses very small or infinitesimal doses of substances derived from plants, minerals or animals to activate the body's nervous system and thereby initiate the healing response. The word 'homeopathy' comes from two Greek words: *homolos* meaning 'similar' and *pathos* meaning 'suffering or disease'.

Homeopathic treatment focuses on the whole person rather than just individual symptoms, it helps to stimulate the body's own natural defence mechanisms. The body has a powerful built-in ability to heal itself and under normal circumstances will maintain a healthy state of well-being. The theory behind homeopathy maintains that the symptoms of a disease represent the body's way of giving us information via the sensory nervous system. We can reinforce the body's efforts to get well by administering small doses of a substance which, if taken in large quantities, might well produce identical symptoms as the disease. Homeopathy is very common and widely accepted in England, France, Switzerland and Germany. It is also used throughout India.

The concepts of homeopathy are:

- To treat the whole person and the source of his or her ailments and not just the symptoms.

- To restore physical, mental and emotional balance and harmony.

- To treat with substances which can produce disease symptoms in large doses, but also cure the disease in small doses.

- To enhance the healing effects of a medicine by diluting, also thereby eliminating the medicine's side effects.

History of homeopathy

A German physician and chemist, Dr Samuel Hahnemann (1755–1843), founded the science of homeopathy. Hahnemann was justifiably distressed about bloodletting, leeching, purging and other medical procedures of the time, maintaining that they did far more harm than good. While researching the toxic effects of medicines during the late 1700s Dr Hahnemann discovered that a specific dilution of a certain substance would remove the symptoms that the same substance was capable of evoking. He then carried out various experiments and confirmed his theory that 'like is cured by like'. Today this is one of the main principles upon which homeopathy is based. The practice of homeopathy spread rapidly through Europe during Hahnemann's lifetime, mostly due to the success of homeopathic physicians in treating cholera during the Napoleonic Wars.

How does homeopathy work?

Samuel Hahnemann discovered the two following laws that govern the science of homeopathy today:

Law of similars

This says that a substance that produces a particular set of symptoms in a healthy person, will cure the same set of symptoms in an unhealthy person.

Law of potentisation

This refers to the particular dilution procedure that all homeopathic remedies go through. With successive shaking the remedies are diluted to various levels called potencies. The lesser dilutions are known as low potencies and the greater dilutions are known as high potencies which act deeper in the nervous system, therefore creating a more potent effect upon the body's natural healing responses.

Another doctor, Constantine Hering (1800–1879), added to Hahnemann's work by discovering a further set of laws that governs homeopathy. He was one of the first to observe specific ways that the healing process develops. He made three observations of the true healing process which have been subsequently been known as Hering's Law of Cure.

Hering's law of cure

THE HUMAN BODY SEEKS TO EXTERNALISE DISEASE.

One of the amazing functions of the body is the capacity to displace a disease from more serious internal levels to more superficial, external levels. After taking a homeopathic remedy, a patient with a long-standing mental or emotional condition may develop new external symptoms such as a skin rash. When this happens, the patient often notices an improvement in their mental or emotional condition. This is contrary to most conventional medical treatments, which would try to control or suppress physical symptoms without treating their cause, thus possibly resulting in the patient's developing more serious symptoms later.

HEALING PROGRESSES FROM THE TOP OF THE BODY TO THE BOTTOM.
A person with a condition that is present over their entire body, may notice relief in the upper body before the lower body. This law of healing helps the homeopath to differentiate a true cure from temporary relief, suppression or a placebo response.

HEALING OCCURS IN THE REVERSE ORDER OF THE APPEARANCE OF THE SYMPTOMS.
As healing occurs, patients may sometimes re-experience symptoms that they have previously suffered from. This aggravation is only experienced for a short period of time (usually a maximum of a few days). After these symptoms disappear the patient feels healthier.

Remedies

Homeopathic remedies are made from plants such as aconite, dandelion and plantain; from minerals such as iron phosphate, arsenic oxide and sodium chloride; from animals such as the venom of a number of poisonous snakes and the ink of the cuttlefish; or even from chemical drugs such as penicillin and streptomycin. They are prepared by a process of repeated dilution and shaking, which makes them capable of stimulating the body's own defence system.

The most common form of homeopathic remedies are little white pellets that dissolve quickly under the tongue. Homeopathic medicines also come in liquid extract, or tincture form and as lotions, ointments, gels and salves that treat external problems like rashes or bruises.

The remedy is usually given once only, and then allowed to work for a long time (sometimes two or three months). Homeopaths recognise the importance of intervening as little as possible. They know the body is intelligent and produces symptoms for a reason. Homeopaths choose a single homeopathic remedy which can strengthen the body's own healing abilities.

After the correct homeopathic remedy, most patients feel a greater sense of well-being and happiness. Homeopathic care goes much deeper than many other types of treatment. After some time (usually between six weeks and two months) the homeopath will want to see you again, to check your physical and emotional changes.

Antidotes

Homeopathic remedies are powerful medicines but they work in such small energetic doses that they can easily be antidoted. The following antidotal guidelines should be heeded for the best results:

AVOID HEAT, LIGHT AND MOISTURE

Keep your homeopathic remedies tightly sealed in a cool, dark place away from moisture.

REFRAIN FROM MINT

Avoid any mint, including peppermint sweets or toothpaste – you can get mint-free toothpaste from most health food stores.

AVOID AROMATICS

Substances like menthol, camphor, tiger balm and perfume can neutralise homeopathic remedies. As a rule it is not beneficial to mix homeopathy with aromatherapy.

DO NOT TOUCH

Pour the remedy pills from the bottle into the cap and from the cap into your mouth, as even the oils from your skin can neutralise the effect of the remedy.

REFRAIN FROM SMOKING, COFFEE AND CAFFEINE

These can neutralise the effect of the homeopathic remedy especially if you drink coffee or smoke within 30 minutes of taking it.

DO NOT TAKE A REMEDY WITH MEALS

Do not eat or drink anything for at least 30 minutes before or after taking a homeopathic remedy.

DO NOT CHEW OR SWALLOW THE PELLETS

Dissolve homeopathic pellets directly underneath your tongue where they can be absorbed quickly into your bloodstream. Homeopathic drops can be taken the same way or in a glass of water.

How soon can results be expected?

In acute conditions, the appropriate homeopathic remedy can work within a few minutes. It is commonplace to see a child, who is screaming with a particular pain, drop off to sleep one to two minutes after a dose of the appropriate homeopathic remedy. In chronic conditions results can be slower. As a rough guide it is thought that for every year a person has suffered from a particular illness it may take a month of treatment to receive maximum results, although some improvement will be noticed in less time. Even though spectacular results often occur, do not be discouraged if there is a delay, particularly if you have been suffering from stress for some time.

Visiting a homeopath

Homeopathy is often very effective for people who experience chronic stress. It may be used to treat long-term physical or emotional problems, as well as recurrent illnesses.

In conventional medicine, you may go to a doctor for a specific disease or problem and you are often prescribed a medicine to make the symptoms of that problem go away. However, according to a homeopathic view, the symptoms are there for a reason, and if the reason is not dealt with then the problem will return at a later date, either in the same form or as a different disease or problem. A homeopath has a clear understanding of the difference between suppression of symptoms and real cure. A cure means that the root of the problem is dealt with, and as a result, the symptoms are no longer needed and fade away.

In most cases homeopaths look not just at the symptoms in isolation, but at everything that is occurring in the patient's life. For example, a patient may come in complaining of headaches, but may also have depression and tiredness as a result of stress. All these problems may stem from the same root cause and by dealing with the cause, it is quite likely that all of the other problems will eventually fade away. During a lengthy initial appointment (often for over an hour) all of the problems will be explored. The homeopath will also take into account your personality and idiosyncrasies as you are talking to them.

Many homeopaths maintain that certain people have a special affinity to a particular remedy (a constitutional remedy) and will respond to it for a variety of ailments. Such remedies can be prescribed according to the person's 'constitutional type' – named after the corresponding remedy. In this way a single homeopathic remedy, matching the whole picture, is chosen.

Homeopathic remedies for stress

This quick reference guide shows common remedies which may be useful for stress. These remedies are available at many chemists and health food shops. This information is not intended to replace the advice of a qualified homeopath. For more personalised, focused remedies, please refer to your local homeopath – addresses of the national homeopathic societies can be found at the back of the book.

ACONITE – This remedy is for those who feel intense anxiety with restlessness often causing insomnia. These people are terror stricken with feelings of foreboding and have a fear of nightmares.

ARGENTUM NITRICUM – For those who are over-anxious. These people are impulsive and hurried yet timid. They dread ordeals or exams and often have many phobias and may wake from frightening dreams.

ARNICA – This is an excellent remedy after mental strain or shock. The fear remains especially at nights causing sleeplessness.

CHAMOMILLA – For those who are impatient, quarrelsome or angry and express dissatisfaction with everything.

GELSEMIUM – For those who have a nervous dread of appearing in public. They cannot cry and are unable to get fully asleep and often wake worrying.

IGNATIA – For those who are oversensitive or nervous after shock, grief or disappointment.

KALI PHOSPHORLAIM – This remedy is for those who suffer from long term worry often causing insomnia. A good remedy for those who are overworked.

NUX VOMICA – For those who are angry, impatient or nervous. They often wake at three or four in the morning, lie awake for hours and then fall into a heavy sleep from which they are reluctant to be aroused.

If any of the above descriptions seem to be appropriate in your situation try a low potency. This will be shown on the bottle as 6c, 12c or 30c. Take one dose three times a day for two or three days. If no improvement occurs, do not continue the medication. If improvement occurs, reduce the dose down to twice a day for 6c and 12c or once a day for 30c and continue for a few more days. Do not take any of the remedies long term unless you are under the direction of a qualified homeopath.

The growing popularity of homeopathy might lead some to think that they don't need to go and see an experienced practitioner. Today, there seem to be homeopathic formulas for most conditions readily available. While these can be helpful in relieving certain acute situations, they are inherently superficial and most likely to be of little lasting value if you are suffering from chronic stress. It is important to remember that remedies that are incorrectly prescribed and are repeatedly taken on a daily basis may actually cause symptoms to appear rather than disappear.

9

affirming yourself

When I was 30 I met a 90-year-old man and I asked him if he could tell me something that he had learnt about life that would help me for my remaining days on this planet. He turned to me, looked me straight in the eye and said:

'I really don't know very much, but it seems to me that these days no one is satisfied with what they have. They all think that the grass is greener on the other side of the fence – but very rarely is it.'

All the healthy diets, the right exercises and the beneficial therapies will not reduce stress permanently unless you are determined to start to enjoy your life for what it is. Helen Keller, the deaf and blind poet, once said that the best and most beautiful things in the world cannot be seen, nor touched, but only felt with the heart. It is because we have forgotten to take the time to listen to what our hearts are saying that we allow stress to strangle happiness out of our lives. At the end of life no one feels really pleased with themselves because they got the children to school on time or that they clinched that business deal or did all that over-time at work, but they do fondly remember the smiling faces and love of their family and friends. They do remember the acts of kindness that they received or happy times that they shared with others. As Ralph Waldo Emerson once wisely pointed out:

'You cannot do a kindness too soon, because you never know how soon will be too late.'

The miracle within

If we are ever to feel the true wonder of life it is essential that we start to glimpse the importance of our existence and start to live from a place of joy, which is our birthright. We need to realise who we really are, rather than believing that we are what everyone else has taught us to be. In our heart of hearts we all know that there is something very wrong with the values and priorities that society has imposed on us. It is up to us to change these beliefs. If we suffer from stress, it is a clear sign that our priorities in life are out of balance and changes are urgently needed. If we have got into stressful habits that have been strongly reinforced over many years we will be out of touch with what we really need and what our hearts are trying to communicate to us. In fact, the very idea of listening to our hearts or intuition will seem alien to us. Although inspiring words, taking remedies or having a massage can help to reduce stress in the short term, nothing will make a big difference until we decide to re-evaluate the priorities in our life. It is a matter of waking up to the realisation that you are the crown of creation and have divinity within you. Once you realise this, nothing will be able to stress you, as everything else will become less important than yourself. It is so often the case that we freely give our valuable time to the trivial things in life while at the same time giving hardly any importance to the things that truly matter.

The old Irish sayings 'you don't see a hearse with a tow-bar' and 'a shroud has no pockets' remind us that we cannot take anything with us from this world. Although this is a sobering thought, it can encourage us to look seriously at our priorities and help us to live life in the present rather than to look to the future for our happiness.

Just before his death, the famous warrior Alexander the Great, who many centuries ago conquered nearly all of the known world, saw the foolishness of his actions and ordered the following epithet to be written on his grave:

'Here lies Alexander the Great, who set out to conquer the whole world, came into this world empty handed and left empty handed.'

Legend has it that he instructed some of his loyal subjects to make sure that his empty hands were extended out from either side of the coffin to demonstrate this fact. He left this important message in the hope that those who came after him would realise the futility of living life for material gain.

Obtaining happiness does not involve grasping at materialism, but weeding out those things in life that prevent the natural inner happiness from emerging. In order to reduce our stress levels there is absolutely nothing that we *need* to do; but there are plenty of behaviour patterns, faulty ways of thinking and judgmental thoughts about ourselves and others that we need to stop doing. When, through conscious choice, we have the ability to refuse to become stressed when demands are placed upon us, we will begin to become aware of how beautiful life can be. This is every human being's right – the only requirements are to be courageous enough to let go of lifelong habits and to have enough determination to refuse to be swept along by the madness of this world. The reward that awaits us is a feeling of love that is right behind each breath that we take. True joy is not a mental or emotional state; it is not something that we feel when one or other of our desires has been satisfied or our goals achieved – it is an awakening of our spirit.

One of my favourite stories is a true account of a lame beggar who lived in India and who slept, ate and begged in exactly the same place each day. He remained in this tragic state for many years, receiving barely enough money to feed himself. One day he died, and because he had no family in the village the local people had to decide what to do with him. After some discussion, they decided to bury him at the very spot where he had spent the last three decades begging, so they started to dig a grave. After a short while they found a large chest crammed full with gold, silver and precious jewels. As it turned out the beggar had spent all his life begging for a few rupees when he was, in fact, sitting on a priceless treasure. In the same way, we also have a priceless treasure – the gift of life – which is the nearest thing to us at all times, but we become stressed and worried because we forget to appreciate it.

Our main priority should be to realise how precious and unique we and our fellow human beings are. Once we start to appreciate our individual qualities we no longer need to compare ourselves with other people, and we will begin to measure our success by what we are rather than by our worldly achievements. As a result, the stress and irritation will be replaced by a deep contentment, inner harmony and love of life. We all have the power within us to alter our consciousness and allow a spontaneous gratitude to unfold. The more aware we are about the true importance of this existence, the less stress, fear and worry we will have in our lives.

By choosing a different response to the demands that are placed on us, we can start to dissolve the mental turmoil and find the inner peace and contentment that is always present. As stress levels are reduced you will be able to reconnect with your true self and get a better sense of who you really are and what you want out of life. In each and every one of us lies the possibility to discover a far greater potential than we can ever imagine. However, it takes great courage to break out of our superimposed defensive shell and welcome the new way of living that will invariably follow.

Freedom of choice

The word 'stress' indicates two forces going in opposite directions; in fact, the dictionary definition of stress is 'to be drawn tight by a system of forces'. A piece of string or a bridge can be under stress when there are two forces acting on it in different directions. There are also two opposing forces acting on us when we feel stressed. These are:

the desire to do what is enjoyable

and

the feeling of obligation to do what we think we have to do.

These are often in direct opposition to one another. Stress therefore seems to occur when we feel we have no choice in a given situation. Any stress-reduction technique that does not endeavour to change our reaction to external stimuli by altering the way in which we think and react will bring only temporary relief.

In Western civilisation, many of us unconsciously live in fear of not having enough time or money. This prevents us from feeling happy and free. Freedom of choice is fundamental to a happy and fulfilled life. When an animal feels trapped it becomes stressed, and the same is true of humans. If you look at a person under stress, you will find that they feel trapped in a situation they believe they are unable to do anything about, and they will often use one of the following words or phrases to describe their plight:

· must	· should	· shouldn't	· got to
· ought to	· ought not	· have to	· can't

All these words which are used frequently when a person is feeling stressed are dis-empowering as they give a person the feeling that there is no choice. Freedom of choice is so important to us that many millions of people have died in countless wars trying to preserve our precious right to choose, yet today this freedom is being subtly eroded away on a daily basis. We may think we are free because we live in a 'free country', but how many of us feel free? Just listen to a person who is stressed talking about their situation and you will probably hear one of these phrases:

- I *should* be at work on time.

- I *must* be going now because otherwise I am going to be late.

- I have *got to* finish this work before tomorrow.

- I *can't* get to my appointment because of the traffic.

- I *have to* cook the meals every day.

- I *ought to* go and do the housework.

If you are under stress at the moment, it might be useful to consider how often you use this type of phraseology when describing your situation.

The reality is that we do have freedom of choice and we need to affirm this in our lives. We are not machines that are set to accomplish a certain task in a particular time. While this may serve employers, businesses or governments – it does not serve you. There is really only one reason why people get stressed and that is that they have low self-confidence because they have forgotten who they really are and what the true purpose of human existence is. We all need to affirm that we deserve peace, love and happiness in our lives.

Some people write or say affirmations over and over again to try to change certain belief systems. But it is not really a belief that needs changing – it is more that we can have a flash of realisation of who we are and what this life could be. The divine within us is our true identity and is patiently waiting for us to stop and realise it. This spirit within never gets stressed, nor hates, nor feels jealousy, nor is greedy, nor is unkind. A condition of continual stress is merely the absence of the feeling of joy within.

The great genius Albert Einstein described our condition well when he said that a human being is part of a whole called by us 'the Universe', a part limited in time and space. A human being experiences himself, his thoughts and feelings, as something separate from the rest; a kind of optical illusion of his consciousness.

This delusion is a kind of prison for us, and what we think we need is restricted to our personal desires and to the affections of a few people nearest to us. Our task must be to free ourselves from this prison by widening our circle of understanding and compassion to embrace all living creatures and the whole of nature and beauty. Just recently I read the following story in *Song of the Bird* by Anthony De Mello that was a clear reflection of Einstein's words:

'There was once a man walking through the wood and he came upon an eagle's egg. He took it home and placed it in a nest of farm hens and waited until it hatched out with the other chicks. For all her life the eagle did exactly the same as the farm chickens, scratching the earth for insects and worms. Thinking that she was a farm-bird, she copied movements and thrashed her wings to fly a foot or two into the air. She even learnt the language of the other chickens and clucked and cackled from sunrise to sunset.

As the years passed, the eagle grew very old and her movements became slow and her clucking more infrequent. One day the old eagle looked into the cloudless blue sky and saw a magnificent bird soaring above. It glided with such graceful poise among the powerful wind currents, scarcely beating its strong golden wings.

The old eagle stared for several minutes completely in awe. "Who is that?" she asked the other chickens. "That is the great eagle – the king of all the birds," said her friends. The old eagle gave a big sigh and settled back into the dust. So it was that the eagle lived and died as a chicken, because that's what she thought she was.'

In the same way our perception of ourselves will rule the way in which we live. This perception has been placed there through our education which is ruled by the belief systems of our society. Reducing those stress levels is simple – it requires that you wake up to the fact that you are an eagle and not a chicken. The only hard thing about it is throwing away all those chicken habits that we have become so accustomed to! W. Somerset Maugham summed it up when he said; 'It's a funny thing about life; if you refuse to accept anything but the best ... you very often get it.'

Today it is not only individuals who are under stress – it seems that the whole planet is. Yet, although the life support systems of the planet are in jeopardy, many people seem to be carrying on like nothing is happening. Woody Allen once said, 'More than at any time in history, mankind faces a crossroads. One path leads to despair and utter hopelessness, the other to total extinction. Let's pray we have the wisdom to choose correctly!' Although this is intended as a joke there is a lot of truth in it. It is vital that we find a third path, another choice, another way of being; one that offers hope and contentment to ourselves and our children – one that avoids the possible disasters that now face mankind in the form of stress-related illnesses, and the global stresses that environmentalists have been warning us about for decades.

Someone sent me the following list of rules, which I found not only amusing, but also helpful in finding a path away from stress towards a more harmonious existence – perhaps you will too.

Rules for being human

YOU WILL RECEIVE A BODY.
You may like it or hate it, but it will be yours for the entire period this time around.

YOU WILL LEARN LESSONS.
You are enrolled in a full-time, informal school called life. Each day in this school you will have the opportunity to learn lessons. You may enjoy the lessons or think them irrelevant and stupid.

THERE ARE NO MISTAKES, ONLY LESSONS.
Growth is a process of trial and error, and experimentation. The 'failed' experiments are just as much a part of the learning process as the experiments that ultimately 'work'.

A LESSON IS REPEATED UNTIL IT IS LEARNED.
A lesson will be presented to you in various forms until you have learned it. Then you can go on to the next lesson.

LEARNING LESSONS DOES NOT END.
There is no part of life that does not contain its lessons. If you are alive, there are lessons to be learned.

PROBLEMS REPLACE PROBLEMS.
Do not be in too much of a hurry to get rid of your problems – once you get rid of one, for sure another will replace it immediately.

'THERE' IS NO BETTER THAN 'HERE'.
When your 'there' has become 'here', you will simply obtain another 'there' that again, looks better than 'here'.

OTHERS ARE MERELY MIRRORS OF YOU.
You cannot love or hate something about another person unless it reflects to you something you love or hate about yourself.

WHAT YOU MAKE OF YOUR LIFE IS UP TO YOU.
You have all the tools and resources you need; what you do with them is up to you. The choice is yours.

THE ANSWERS LIE INSIDE YOU.
The answers to life's questions lie inside you. All you need to do is look, listen and trust.

YOU WILL FORGET ALL THIS.
You might find it helpful to ponder on each of these rules for a day – you will get insights.

I would like to leave you with 12 suggestions for an easier life. Slowing down and simplifying life is the only sure way that we can truly realise the importance of this existence and how special we are.

1. Never judge a day by the weather

2. The best things in life aren't things

3. Tell the truth – there is less to remember

4. Speak softly, act loudly

5. Read something funny at least once a day

6. Learn to laugh at yourself – you will have a lifetime's worth of humour

7. Goals are deceptive – the unaimed arrow never misses

8. The more you accumulate in life, the more you have to leave behind

9. Age is relative – when you are 'over the hill' you begin to pick up speed

10. There are two ways to be rich – make more money or desire less

11. Internal beauty increases with age – external looks are illusionary

12. No rain – no rainbows!

useful addresses

Richard Brennan
Richard Brennan runs weekend and week-long courses on how to reduce stress using the Alexander Technique in Ireland, UK, Spain and Greece.
Richard Brennan
The Alexander Technique Training Centre
Kirkullen Lodge
Tooreeny
County Galway
Ireland
E-mail: rickbrennan@eircom.net
Internet: http://homepage.eircom.net/~alexandertechnique

Stress Relief with the Alexander Technique Self-Help Audio Cassette
This is the perfect accompaniment to this book and gives clear and concise instructions on:
· How to eliminate unwanted tension
· How to prevent or relieve back pain
· How to improve your breathing
· How to reduce your stress levels
· How to clear your mind from unwanted thoughts
· How to practise the two Alexander principles of Inhibition and Direction
· How to stay in the present moment.

The cost of the audio cassette is £11 or US$20. It can be ordered direct from Richard Brennan at the address above.

For a list of practitioners or full details of any of the therapies in your area please send a stamped addressed envelope to one of the following addresses:

Acupuncture
UK
British Acupuncture Council
Park House
206–208 Latimer Road
London W10 6RE
Tel: 0208 964 0222

British Medical Acupuncture Society
Newton House
Newton Lane
Whitley
Warrington WA4 4JA
Tel: 01925 730727
Internet:
http~llusers.aol.corn/acubmas.bmas.ht
inf

Ireland
Acupuncture Foundation of Ireland
Dominick Court
41 Lower Dominick Street
Dublin
Tel: 01 662 3525

USA
American Association of Oriental
Medicine
433 Front Street
Catasauqua
PA 18032-2506
Tel: (610) 266 1433
Fax: 264 2768
E-mail: AAOM1@aol.com
Internet: www.aaom.org/

National Acupuncture and Oriental
Medicine Alliance
PO Box 77511
Seattle
WA 98177
Tel: 206 524 3511
E-mail: 76143.2061@compuserve.com

Australia
Australian Acupuncture and Chinese
Medicine Association
PO Box 5142

West End
QLD 4101
Internet: www.acupuncture.org.au/

Alexander Technique
UK
Alexander Technique International
UK Regional Co-ordinator
66c Thurlestone Road
London SE27 0PD
Tel: 07071 880253
Internet: www.ati-net.com

The Society of Teachers of the
Alexander Technique
20 London House
266 Fulham Road
London SW10 9EL
Tel: 0207 351 0828
Internet: www.stat.org.uk

Ireland
Alexander Technique International
Kirkullen Lodge
Tooreeny
County Galway
Tel/Fax: 091 555800
Internet: www.ati-net.com

USA
Alexander Technique International Inc
1692 Massachusetts Avenue
3rd Floor
Cambridge
Boston
MA 02138
Tel: 617 497 2242
Fax: 617 497 2615
E-mail: usa@ati-net.com
Internet: www.ati-net.com

The North American Society of
Teachers of the Alexander Technique
PO Box 112484
Tacoma
WA 98411-2484
Tel: 612 824 5066
Internet: www.alexandertech.org/

Australia
Alexander Technique International
11/11 Stanley Street
Darlinghurst
NSW 2010
Tel: 02 3331 7563
Internet: www.ati-net.com

The Australian Society of Teachers of
the Alexander Technique
PO Box 716
Darlinghurst
NSW 2010
Tel: 0398 531356
E-mail: tfitzgerald@ozemail.com.au

Aromatherapy
UK
Aromatherapy Organisations Council
3 Latymer Close
Braybrooke
Market Harborough
Leicestershire LE16 8LN
Tel: 01858 434242

Aromatherapy Trade Council
PO Box 52
Market Harborough
Leicestershire LE16 8ZX

Ireland
Irish and International Aromatherapy
Association
Roscore
Blueball
Tullamore
County Offaly

USA
National Association for Holistic
Aromatherapy
PO Box 17622
Boulder
CO 80308

National Association for Holistic
Aromatherapy
836 Hanley Industrial Court
St Louis
MO 63144
Tel: 314 963 2071
Fax: 314 963 4454

E-mail: info@naha.org
Internet: www.naha.org

Australia
International Federation of
Aromatherapy
PO Box 2210
Central Park
VIC 3145
E-mail: membership@ifa.org.au
Internet: www.ifa.org.au/

Bach Flower Remedies
UK
The Dr Edward Bach International
Centre
Mount Vernon
Bakers Lane
Sotwell
Wallingford OX10 0PZ
Tel: 01491 834678
Internet: www.bachcentre.com

Chinese Herbal Medicine
UK
Register of Chinese Herbal Medicine
PO Box 400
Wembley
London HA9 9NZ
Tel: 0208 904 1357

USA
American Association of Oriental
Medicine
433 Front Street
Catasauqua
PA 18032 2506
Tel: (610) 266 1433
Fax: 264 2768
E-mail: AAOM1@aol.com

National Acupuncture and Oriental
Medicine Alliance
PO Box 77511
Seattle
WA 98177
Tel: 206 524 3511
E-mail: 76143.2061@compuserve.com

Australia
Australian Acupuncture and Chinese
Medicine Association

PO Box 5142
West End
QLD 4101
Internet: www.Acupuncture.org.au/

Chiropractic
UK
British Chiropractic Association
29 Whitley Street
Reading RG2 0EG
Tel: 0118 757557

McTimoney Chiropractic Association
21 High Street
Eynsham OX8 1HE
Tel: 01865 880974

Scottish Chiropractic Association
30 Roseburn Place
Edinburgh EH12 5NX
Tel: 0131 346 7500

Ireland
Chiropractic Association of Ireland
Roscarn
Merlin Park
County Galway
Tel: 091 751858

USA
American Chiropractic Association
1701 Clarendon Blvd
Arlington
VA 22209
Tel: 800 986 4636
Fax: 703 243 2593
Internet: http://amerchiro.org

Australia
Chiropractic Association of Australia
459 Great Western Highway
Faulconbridge
NSW 2776
Internet: www.caa.com.au/

Feldenkrais
UK
The Feldenkrais Guild
PO Box 370
London N10 3XA
Tel: 07000 785506
Internet: www.feldenkrais.co.uk

USA
The Feldenkrais Guild of North
America
3611 S.W. Hood Ave
Suite 100
Portland
OR 97201
Tel: 800 775 2118
Internet: www.feldenkrais.com/

Herbal Medicine
UK
National Institute of Medical Herbalists
56 Longbrook Street
Exeter EX4 6AH
Tel: 01392 426022
Fax: 01392 498963
Internet:
http://guest.btinternet.com/index.shtml

USA
American Herbalists Guild
PO Box 70
Roosevelt
UT 84066
Tel: 435 722 8434
Fax: 435 722 8452
E-mail: ahgoffice@earthlink.net
Internet: www.healthy.net/herbalists/

Australia
National Herbalists Association of
Australia
Suite 305
PO Box 61
BST House
Broadway
NSW 2007
Tel: 02 9211 6437
Fax: 02 9211 6452
E-mail: nhaa@nhaa.org.au
Internet: www.nhaa.org.au

Homeopathy
UK
British Homeopathic Association
27a Devonshire Street
London W1N 1RJ
Tel: 0207 935 2163

Faculty of Homeopathy
2 Powis Place
Great Ormond Street
London WCIN 3HT
Tel: 0207 837 9469

Society of Homeopaths
2 Artizan Road
Northampton NN1 4HU
Tel: 01604 621400
E-mail:
societyofhomeopaths@btinternet.com
Internet: www.homeopathy.org.uk

Ireland

Irish Society of Homeopaths
66 Mount Anville Wood
Goatstown
Dublin 14
Tel: 01 278 3161

Irish Society of Homeopaths
35–37 Ruxton Court
Dominick Street
County Galway
Tel/Fax: 091 563040
E-mail: ishom@eircom.ie

Irish Medical Homeopathic
Association
16 Oaklands
Ballsbridge
Dublin 4
Tel: 01 668 9242

USA

North American Society of
Homeopaths (NASH)
2024 S Dearborn St
Seattle
WA 98144
Fax: 206 329 5684
E-mail: nashinfo@aol.com
Internet: www.homeopathy.org

Australia

Australian Homeopathic Association
PO Box 396
Drummoyne
NSW 2047
E-mail: georgec@mailbox.uq.edu.au

Hypnotherapy
UK

British Society of Experimental and
Clinical Hypnosis
c/o Dept of Psychology
Grimsby General Hospital
Scartho Road
Grimsby DN33 2BA
Tel: 01472 879238

British Society of Medical and Dental
Hypnosis (England)
17 Keppel View Road
Kimberworth
Rotherham S61 2AR
Tel: 01709 554558

British Society of Medical and Dental
Hypnosis (Scotland)
PO Box 1007
Glasgow G31 2LE
Tel: 0141 556 1606

National School of Hypnotherapy and
Psychotherapy
The Central Register of Advanced
Hypnotherapists
28 Finsbury Park Road
London N4 2JX
Tel: 0207 359 6991

Ireland

Irish Institute of Counselling and
Hypnotherapy
118 Stillorgan Road
Dublin 4
Tel: 01 260 0118

Irish Association of Hypno-analysts
Therapy House
6 Tuckey Street
Cork
Tel: 021 275 785

USA

National Board for Certified Clinical
Hypnotherapists
Suite142E
8750 Georgia Avenue
Silver Spring
MD 20901
Tel: 800 449 8144
Fax: 301 588 9535

E-mail: nbcch@natboard.com
Internet: www.natboard.com/

Massage
UK
British Massage Therapy Council
Greenbank House
65a Adelphi Street
Preston PR1 7BH
Tel: 01772 881063

Massage Therapy Institute of Great
Britain
PO Box 2726
London NW2 4NR
Tel: 0208 208 1607

Ireland
The Irish Massage Therapists
Association
Ard Lynn
Mount Rice
Monasterevin
County Kildare
Tel: 045 525 579

USA
Associated Bodywork and Massage
Professionals
28677 Buffalo Park Road
Evergreen
CO 80439
Tel: 800 458 2267
Fax: 303 674 0859
E-mail: expectmore@abmp.com
Internet: www.abmp.com/

Meditation
UK
Friends of the Western Buddhist Order
London Buddhist Centre
51 Roman Road
London E2 0HU
Tel: 0208 9811225

School of Meditation
158 Holland Park Avenue
London W11 4UH
Tel: 0207 603 6116

Transcendental Meditation
Freepost

London SWIP 4YY
Tel: 0990 143733
Internet: www.maharishi.com.uk

USA
Dharma Net International
3115 San Ramon Road
Concord
CA 94519
E-mail: dharma@dharmanet.org
Internet: www.dharmanet.org

Australia
Vipassana Meditation Centre
PO Box 103
Blackheath
NSW 2785
Tel: 02 4787 7436
Fax: 02 4787 7221
E-mail: info@bhumi.dhamma.org
Internet: www.dhamma.org

Osteopathy
UK
General Council and Register of
Osteopaths
56 London Street
Reading RG1 4SQ
Tel: 0118 957 6585

Guild of Osteopaths
497 Bury New Road
Prestwich
Manchester M25 1AD
Tel: 0161 798 6352

Osteopathic Information Service
PO Box 2074
Reading RG1 4YR
Tel: 0118 951 2051

Ireland
The Irish Osteopathic Association
17 Windsor Terrace
Portobello
Dublin 8
Tel: 01 473 0828

USA
American Osteopath Association
142 E Ontario Street
Chicago
IL 60611

Tel: 800 621 1773
Fax: 312 202 8000
Internet: www.am.osteo-assn.org/

The American Academy of Osteopathy
Suite 1080
3500 DePauw Blvd
Indianapolis
Indiana 46268
Tel: 317 879 1881
Fax: 317 879 0563

Australia

Australian Osteopathic Association
PO Box 242
Thornleigh
NSW 2120
Tel: 02 9980 8511
Fax: 02 9980 8466
E-mail: aoa@tpgi.com.au
Internet: www.osteopathic.com.au/

Qi Gong
UK

Lamas Qigong Association
25 Watson Road
Worksop
Nottinghamshire S80 2BA
Tel/Fax: 01909 482190 & 01909 482156
E-mail: LAMASQI@aol.com
Internet: http://www.lamas.org/

USA

National Qi Gong Association
PO Box 540
Ely
Min 55731
Tel: 888 233 3655
Internet: http//www.nga.org/

Australia

Golden Lion Academy
94 High Street
Berwick
Victoria 3806
Tel: 3 9796 1066
Fax: 3 9796 2388
E-mail: pcr@goldlion.com.au
Internet: http://www.goldlion.com.au

Reflexology
UK

Association of Reflexologists
27 Old Gloucester Street
London WC1 3XX
Tel: 0990 673320

British Reflexology Association
Monks Orchard
Whitbourne
Worcester WR6 5RB
Tel: 01886 821207

Ireland

The Irish Reflexologists Institute (IRI)
3 Blackglen Court
Lambs Cross
Sandyford
Dublin 18
Tel: 01 295 2238

USA

Reflexology Association of America
4012 Rainbow Street
K-PMB 585
Las Vegas
NV 89103 2059
Internet: www.reflexology-usa.org/

International Council of Reflexologists
PO Box 17356
San Diego
CA 92177 7356
Tel: 619 275 1011
E-mail:interncouncilreflex@juno.com

Australia

International Council of Reflexologists
PO Box 1032
Bondi Junction
NSW 1355
Tel: 61 2 9300 9391
Fax: 61 2 9300 9216
Internet: www.reflexologyworld.com

Shiatsu
UK

Shiatsu Society
31 Pullman Lane
Godalming GU7 lXY
Tel: 01483 860771

Ireland
The Shiatsu Society of Ireland
12 The Cove
Malahide
Dublin
Tel: 01 845 3647

USA
International School of Shiatsu
10 South Clinton Street
Doylestown
PA 18901
Tel: 215 340 9918
Fax: 215 340 9181
E-mail: info@shiatsubo.com

Australia
Shiatsu Therapy Association of Australia
PO Box 598
Belgrave 3160
Tel/Fax: 03 9752 6711

Shiatsu Australia Educational Services
PO Box 2064
St Kilda West
Victoria 3182
Tel: 03 9534 4780
Fax: 03 9534 4785
Internet: www.shiatsu.aimtec.net.au

T'ai Chi
UK
T'ai Chi Union for Great Britain
23 Oakwood Avenue
Mitcham CR4 3DQ

Ireland
T'ai Chi Chaun Association
St Andrew's Resource Centre
114–116 Pearse Street
Dublin 2
Tel: 01 677 1930

USA
T'ai Chi Association
4651 Roswell Rd
Buckhead
Atlanta
GA 30342
Tel: 404 289 5652
E-mail: information@tai-chi-association.com

Australia
Taoist T'ai Chi Society of Australia Inc
PO Box 23
Palmyra
WA 6157
Tel/Fax 08 9339 1331
E-Mail: taotai@nettrek.com.au
Internet: www.taoist.org.au/

Yoga
UK
The British Wheel of Yoga
1 Hamilton Place
Boston Road
Sleaford NG34 7ES
Tel: 01529 306851

Ireland
Irish Yoga Association
108 Lower Kimmage Rd
Harold's Cross
Dublin 6
Tel: 01 492 9213

USA
The American Yoga Association
PO Box 19986
Sarasota
Florida 34276
Tel: 941 927 4977
Fax: 941 921 9844
E-mail: YOGAmerica@aol.com
Internet:
http://users.aol.com/amyogssnna/

International Association of Yoga
Therapists
PO Box 1386
Lower Lake
CA 95457
Tel: 707 928 9898
Fax: 707 928 4738

Australia
Australian Institute of Yoga
7/71 Ormond Road
Elwood
Victoria 3184
Tel: 03 9525 6951
E-mail: yogather@hotkey.net.au
Internet: www.hotkey.net.au/

index